"We talk a lot about aging hereabouts, but it's always a boon to hear a first-person account. Ms. Kugel's blog mixes the quotidian and the quietly dramatic."
  Paula Spahn, the *New York Times*

"This thoughtful tour through Judy Kugel's seventies shows how the core findings of extensive research - that aging well is driven by rich social networks and meaningful work or community engagement - play out in day-to-day life. Her insights, drawn from experiences ranging from family and friends to travel and technology, provide an easy-to-read guide to well-being in one's eighth decade, and beyond."
  John W. Rowe, M.D., Co-Author of *Successful Aging*

"I so look forward to Judy Kugel's 70-something blog entries and often find myself forwarding them to friends of all ages. Her many insights on the joys and tribulations of her eighth decade are very candid, occasionally sad or wistful, frequently very funny and always well-written. From my perspective, Judy is a pioneer, slightly ahead of me on the aging curve. The breadth of her experiences and the joy with which she greets them, even the difficult ones, give me hope and confidence as I contemplate the rest of my 70's and beyond. Thank you, Judy!"
  Joseph Quinn, Professor of Economics, Boston College

"As a long-time avid and admiring reader of Judy Kugel's 70-something blog, I celebrate the arrival of her book containing the best of her postings, organized by topics with thoughtful introductions. Now we'll have at hand her always insightful, sometimes poignant, often humorous gems as a friendly companion on our journey into and through elderhood."
  Meg Newhouse, PhD., author of *Legacies of the Heart: Living a Life That Matters,* founder of the Life Planning Network.

Blog readers weigh in too:

"You're a strong writer, but it's more than that. You face challenges with grace and you love with all your heart. It's an inspiration!" MW

"I have been reading your Blog for more years than I'll admit - (OK-maybe 5 or 6) - and it is the best thing ever! I read a lot of blogs ... and yours is awesome and inspiring. Thank you for being a inspiration to a late blooming 50 something." LI

"I rarely comment, but just want to say how much I enjoy your blog. Every Monday and Friday morning, I feel a little twitch of happiness when I see it in my email. Thanks so very much!" KR

"Congratulations on your blog's anniversary! I've really enjoyed reading your blog. I am exactly half your age (in my mid-30s), but as a married mom of two young boys, I savor your wisdom about sustaining a long, happy marriage; raising kind, successful kids; and working for years at a job you really enjoy." RM

70-SOMETHING

LIFE, LOVE AND
LIMITS IN THE BONUS YEARS.

JUDY F. KUGEL

Publisher's Information

EBookBakery Books

Author contact: judy.kugel@gmail.com

ISBN 978-1-938517-68-6

© 2017 by Judy F. Kugel

ACKNOWLEDGMENTS

There would have been no 70-something blog (and therefore no book) without my elder son, Seth Kugel, who challenged me to share journal entries about my eighth decade with the public. Because he impressed me with the importance of writing consistently, I never missed a Thursday or Sunday post.

Our younger son Jeremy Kugel, his amazing wife Katrina and their boys, Leo and Grady are a constant source of inspiration and the subject of many blog posts. They keep me laughing. I can't get enough of them.

I do not have the words to thank my husband and number one reader, Peter Kugel, to whom this book is dedicated. His once-a-year blog posts were highlights for so many. He always has my back.

My dear friends, too many to name, were my first subscribers and they have loyally stayed with me over the years. Thanks guys. Fortunately, they were joined by many readers, male and female, young and old, miraculously from many countries, who often tell me that I "get" how they are feeling. I've loved hearing from them.

The writing was easy. The transition to a real book was hard. For that I thank my publisher Michael Grossman who made it happen. His guidance, his talent, his professionalism and his good humor made working with him a great pleasure.

DEDICATION

For Peter

CONTENTS

PREFACE

A month before my seventieth birthday, I started a blog. I wanted to record my journey through the upcoming decade. It would be about my seventies, for sure. But I also wanted to write about my friends' seventies, my husband's eighties, my sons' forties and my grandchildren's pre-teen years. But mostly, about my seventies.

A decade earlier, I kept an old-fashioned journal to document the last year of my fifties, which I saw as the end of my relative youth. I was dreading my sixties.

But I was wrong. My sixties turned out to be exactly the opposite of dreadful. Our children were educated, my career was chugging along at a fine pace, my health was excellent and the future was bright. My husband Peter and I traveled extensively, mostly by bicycle. I studied Spanish for the first time, had an op-ed published in "*The New York Times*" and several travel articles in magazines and papers. I discovered a half-sister I never knew about it and I became a grandparent.

Most seventy-year-olds don't blog. As far as I knew in January, 2008, seventy-year-olds didn't read blogs either. I hoped that at least my family and a few friends would stick with me. As it turned out, quite a few other people started to read and respond. I was sure they would all be in their 60's or 70's, but a young newly-wed wrote that she is "taking lessons about marriage from me." I heard from 40- and 50-year-olds anticipating their "senior" years. Much to my surprise, I heard from lots of male readers. I've been thanked (mostly) chided (infrequently) and taught (often) by my readers.

On January 10, 2008, my first blog post promised that I would write about parents and parenting, exercise, aging and more. "More" turned out to be whatever was on my mind on the day I wrote, including marriage, work, retirement and friendships. I had quite a bit to say about my body (becoming less "perfect") and health (staying pretty good) because those have a way of attracting your attention as you age. I wrote about travel and food because I take pleasure in both. I love celebrations so birthdays and Thanksgivings got plenty of attention. And so did technology because I was attempting to keep up with it.

I wrote about work while I was still working. I wrote about the transition to not working (aka "retirement") when I left the job I had loved for thirty-three years.

It wasn't until well into my seventies that end-of-life issues appeared in my blog posts. Those of us lucky enough to make it into our eighth decade can expect to have many good years in front of us, but life goes faster when so much is behind you.

I didn't write enough about purpose, something we all search for and may not even recognize when we've found it. I touched on do-overs, but really didn't emphasize enough that we don't get many second chances. Life is not a rehearsal.

I come from the pre-women's-lib generation. I did read Gloria Steinem, Betty Friedan and other feminist authors, but I have remained pretty much a child of the 50's, the so-called "Silent Generation". I was one of the first of my friends with children to have a full-time job, and I worried every day that I wasn't there to greet the kids when they came home after school. I suspect I might have done things differently had I been born five years later. At the least, I would have had an earlier start on my career. No regrets, just an observation.

My generation is lucky to have lived in a time of great prosperity and opportunity. But now we face an uncertain (and shorter) future with its inevitable losses. We must plan for when we may not be able to live independently. It is important that we must make the most of the time we have left.

I've tried to stay positive in my blog. When I was in danger of sounding grumpy, I could hear my mother's voice reminding me, a moody teenager, "Nobody likes a sourpuss." But although I never said outright that I was miserable, this decade has had its challenges. Luckily my seventies brought more to celebrate than I had anticipated.

As I face my ninth decade, I am trying to worry less because I recognize what a waste of time worrying is. I plan to appreciate what I can do and remember, when I'm feeling losses, that we had our time. I accept what and who I am. We only get one run in the marathon of life. I'm slowing down a little, but grateful to still be in the race.

1

NEXT OF KIN

Family

"Family is not an important thing. It's everything."
Michael J. Fox

My family is the center of my universe, always has been, always will be.

If there is any theme to my family blog entries, it's love and pride, and a sense of how lucky we have been as a family. Over the years, I have seen friends with kid problems, including the worst nightmare of all, losing a child. Not to say that I've never had a sleepless night worrying about ours. Not to say that I am not irrationally sad every time we end a visit with our children. But so, so grateful for what we have, and never-ever taking it for granted.

Family is not just the four of us. Our parents are present in us and we are present in our children and grandchildren. Our sisters and brothers, our aunts and uncles and cousins have shared our lives. Our daughter-in-law has become our daughter. They are a part of who we are and they too are family.

We moved often when I was a young child while my father struggled to find his "place" in the work world. I was conceived in Dayton, Ohio and born in Maplewood, New Jersey. We left there when I was ten weeks old to move to Buffalo, New York. We spent four years there, followed by five years in Cincinnati, Ohio before we finally settled in Pittsburgh, Pennsylvania when I was nine. My mother took these moves in stride, but it couldn't have been easy for her.

We've never lived close to extended family, and I am envious of those who do, despite that sometimes being a mixed blessing. I moved to Boston after college and never went back to live in Pittsburgh. I understand now how hard that was for my parents. Our children missed out on having grandparents deeply involved in their lives because they were so far away. I would be thrilled to have our kids closer to us. But not too close, say a 30-minute drive away. Although they are not nearby, we try to be a presence in our grandchildren's lives by traveling to see them as often as we can. It's never enough.

I regret that I cannot ask my parents how they felt as they grew older and what in retrospect they might have done differently when they were my age. Our children don't ask us those questions. And I understand that and hope that one day, they will find answers to their questions in these words.

January 14, 2008

AM I MY MOTHER?

My mother, Lillian Kahn Faskow, was born in Buffalo, New York on the day Wilbur and Orville Wright flew the world's first successful airplane, the Wright Flyer, at Kitty Hawk. (Imagine how they would feel if plopped down in Logan Airport in 2008!) For those of you who haven't heard that date as often as I have over the years, it was December 17, 1903. Note: I've never been to Kitty Hawk, but I enjoyed all the hoopla on the 100th anniversary four years ago.

Mom was one of six children, and she didn't have all the advantages I've enjoyed in life—like a college education, lots of travel and a fulfilling career. However, she and her siblings were a great bunch, and I could write endless blog posts with tales of that clan.

Growing up, when people told me I looked like Mom, I couldn't really see it, but I knew she was pretty and so I always said "thank you". But I shall never forget how shocked I was by an event that occurred while visiting her in her concrete-skyscraper-Florida-beach-front-apartment. I was in the elevator after running an errand when a perfect stranger stepped in. Without missing a beat, she said, "Why you must be Lillian's daughter!"

Comments like that became rather frequent over the years, but it wasn't until I caught a certain angle's glimpse of myself in a bathroom mirror one day, that I was struck by how much I really do look like my mother. Am I my mother redux?

On her visits, Mom always wanted to be helpful. She would ask if I had any mending she could do. She enjoyed keeping her hands busy while watching some sports event with her grandsons. At some point she began asking me to thread the needle for her. It was easy with my young eyes, and I didn't think twice about it.

Mom died in 1989 when she was almost 86 years old.

Last month Peter and I were visiting Seth in New York City. We had been to a theatre matinee, and were going to order in dinner at his co-op so we could watch a New England Patriots playoff game. In the afternoon, I had noticed that the lining of his overcoat was hanging a bit, and I offered to fix it. We stopped on the way home to buy some thread.

While he and his father concentrated on the game, I mended his overcoat. I was too stubborn (proud?) to ask him to thread the needle for me so I struggled to do it myself.

February 1, 2008

FROM GENERATION TO GENERATION

Several years ago, Jeremy asked Peter and me to write about our lives up to the time he was born. So we did. We enjoyed trying to capture the essence of our growing up and the patterns of behavior we developed that made us who we are today, for better or for worse.

We were surprised that each of our hastily written "early-years" autobiographies ended up to be seventeen single-spaced pages long, and that we learned things about each other from reading about our lives before we met.

Then last spring, Jeremy asked us to talk about where we are in our lives on videotape. The plan was that the tapes would be embargoed with no one having watched them until it was played for our grandchildren in 20 years. Jeremy set up the camera, left me, saying he would be back in 15 minutes and instructed me to talk. By the time he came back, I was reduced to tears, telling the video camera how much I loved everyone.

I have no idea what Peter said on his recording, but I do know that he had more trouble filling the 15 minutes than I did, typical silent-male that he is.

I often wish I could talk to my parents these days. I want to know what they were thinking at my age. How did they feel about turning 70? I want to know more about my father's difficult childhood. I want to know if my mother ever wished that she had had a career other than as a mom. I wonder if she had that empty feeling in the pit of her stomach that I always have when a child leaves after a visit home.

Through our writing about our early lives and our recording about where we are now, our children will have answers to some of the questions I wish I could ask my parents. And maybe, just maybe, our grandkids will tell their own children what life was like for their grandparents at the turn of the 21st century.

July 7, 2008

BECKET

Our boys attended a YMCA camp in the Berkshires starting at age ten. We chose Becket because it focused on developing character rather than competitiveness. Although we prefer not to take credit or blame for the people our children are, we do thank Camp Becket for its help.

Both boys attended for years. In Seth's last year, he served as a village director, overseeing a group of counselors, and Jeremy took a summer leave from his after-college-job to lead a group of Becket campers to China in Summer, 1997.

Since we are currently vacationing together in the Berkshires, a half-hour away from Becket, Jeremy arranged a visit. After all, in six more years, his son could be going there.

Our visit brought back the anxiety of leaving a first-born to someone else's care, of the worry when at age fifteen Seth went off to work with fellow campers in a tiny village in Kenya for a summer and then Jeremy at fifteen to Sweden and Russia for a summer of service.

So much was the same—the sailboats, the foursquare courts, cabins with no electricity, no I-pods or email allowed. Just boys being boys.

The camp director invited us to lunch in the dining hall, and a fellow camper of Seth's who is now the camp pediatrician joined us. During the after-lunch announcements, we were welcomed and introduced as heroes (well, the kids were the heroes). The campers erupted in cheers.

Becket looked much as it did 28 years ago when we dropped off Seth. We, of course, are very different.

September 7, 2008

FROM FUSSY EATER TO PHILANTHROPIST

Our son Jeremy was a fussy eater as a child. We had a small mucky-green-colored skillet in which we fried up a nightly hamburger for him. Now that he's grown, he eats just about everything in sight. He has never met a piece of red meat that he didn't like and can down chicken nuggets with the best of them. He recently competed with his boss to see who could gain more weight from eating churrasco, and snuck a scale into a restaurant to battle it out. They weighed themselves before and after. Jeremy gained six pounds.

But for the month of September, 2008, Jeremy is a vegetarian. Here's why. In 2003, Jeremy's friend Yutaka started Excel Academy, a tuition-free public charter school serving underperforming middle school students in East Boston and Chelsea, Massachusetts. It was named Charter School of the Year in 2007 by the Center for Education Reform. Like all nonprofits, it relies on contributions to supplement its meager budget.

This month, Jeremy has a bet with anyone who pledges money to Excel. It works like this. People mail checks, made out to Excel Academy to him. If he eats a morsel of meat in September the checks will be returned. His meatless September hasn't been easy so far, but he has $3,300 in pledges.

If this sounds like a shameless plug for Excel and Jeremy, it's because it is.

December 11, 2008

HOUSE RULES

When our boys were small, they would wolf down their peanut butter or bologna sandwiches (crusts removed) and attack the Oreos. A half-a-bag later, they had enough, but I had to buy more cookies. So Peter and I made a rule— a limit of two cookies for dessert at lunch, three at dinner.

We had some other rules too. Soft drinks only at the weekend "Coketail" hour, the sugar cereal of your choice once a year on your birthday, three pieces of candy per night until the Halloween loot was gone and no candy in the house the rest of the year.

Additional rules included one hour of TV on school nights, everything off the bedroom floor if the cleaning men were coming (on the bed was OK), a three sentence thank you note for all gifts as follows:

1. Thank you for the birthday check
2. I will spend it on_____
3. Hope to see you soon.

Our daughter-in-law Katrina says they had no soda at all in their home growing up. They did not have a TV except when they rented one to watch the Olympics or presidential debates. They never had sugar cereals.

So I wonder what the "house rules" are now in these days of cell phones, laptops, electronic games, text messages, high def. TV and friends with benefits.

Our grandchildren are two and five. They don't get dessert if they don't finish their dinner. That's a good start.

December 12, 2008

BURSTING WITH PRIDE

Possibly the only thing more boring than other people's grandchildren is other people's children. But today is one of those times I can't resist.

The New York Times Travel section today contains Seth's 130th and final *"Weekend in New York"* column. For two-and-a-half years of Sundays, we could turn to the Travel section, see his byline and marvel at his knowledge of that great city.

Today we read how he caught up on some "must do" New York activities that he had missed in his 15 years of living there, like seeing Radio City Music Hall's Rockettes and being in the audience of the David Letterman Show.

More important to us, for the first time he was allowed to write in the first person, and there is a big photo of him on his first visit to the Metropolitan Opera.

Within days of completing this last column, he moved to Brazil to write from South America.

He had a great run

September 9, 2009

BEST DAYS

I decided to make a list of the ten best days of my life. I didn't think about it very much because I've probably had hundreds of "best days." And I expect that if my good luck continues, I'll have a lot more. So here are the "first" top ten.

1. The birth of my son Seth
2. The birth of my son Jeremy
3. Biking to the top of Mt. Constitution on Orcas Island (four miles and eighty hairpin switchbacks) without stopping
4. Seth at twenty-one, presiding over "assembly" with all his counselors and campers as Village Director at Camp Becket.
5. Peter's 65th birthday when Seth's "gift" was a surprise scavenger hunt leading us to places from Peter's childhood years in New York City
6. Jeremy as the hilarious emcee at our twenty-fifth anniversary party
7. Seth teaching his 3rd grade bi-lingual class in the South Bronx about immigration and having Peter talk about his experience as an immigrant
8. Our day with Jeremy in Cerro Navio, a poor district in Santiago, Chile, where he was teaching micro-lending so that the women could start a business to sell their empanadas.
9. Seth and Jeremy attempting to scare us by roaring like hippopotamuses in the bushes below our open cabin as we tried to fall asleep in a camp on Lake Kenai in Zimbabwe in 2000.
10. Publishing my first (and only) op-ed in *The New York Times*

Looks like eight out of ten of my best days were because I'm a mother.

December 6, 2009

Dinner for Just the Four of Us

Until Seth went away to college, dinner was a command performance. We had some standard meals that worked for everyone. Not a week went by without Rice Krispie chicken or hamburgers (cooked outside no matter what the temperature). When the kids were in high school, sports practice may have determined the hour we ate, but never whether we ate together.

Those days seem like ancient history. Except for two years ('95-'97), the children haven't lived in the same town as we have since college, and the four of us without guests or family just never happens. Except for last Sunday. Jeremy's family had left for Maryland, but he stayed over for a business appointment, and Seth wasn't leaving for Brazil for a couple of days. That left the four of us, just like old times.

I felt like I was giving a dinner party. I prepared marinated flank steak. Peter made polenta. We lit candles and had a glass of wine. We all commented about how long it had been and how unusual it was to be just us.

July 4, 2010

My Older Brother Don

I worshipped my tall, handsome, smart and popular older brother throughout high school, even though I found it annoying that everyone always asked me if I was Don's little sister.

He and I haven't lived in the same city for more than fifty years, and our lives have taken quite different turns. He has been married to his third wife for thirty-two years, is a relatively conservative businessman and is still working at seventy-five. I married once, am pretty liberal, and like him, still working, but in academia.

We hadn't seen each other for more than four years when he and his wife Nancy agreed to join us at our beach vacation with our grandkids and their parents. Don's kids are considerably older than ours as are his grandchildren, and I thought he might be a reluctant visitor.

Much to my surprise and delight, Don seemed to have a good time.

He thoroughly charmed our three- and six- year- old grandsons for three days.

Watching them climb all over him on the last night of his visit, cuddling with him on an oversized chair was right up there with the best moments of my year.

December 29, 2010

Snuggly

When our son Seth was an infant, someone gave him Snuggly. Bright orange, soft and cuddly, it seemed reasonable to put it in the crib with our first-born. Little did we know that it would get frequently misplaced and we would spend a considerable portion of our lives as young parents looking for "Gee". Seth would not go to bed without it. If we went away, so did Gee.

At some point, Snuggly was worn out. Fortunately, Peter and I were able to buy a new one. Late one night we snuck into Seth's room and made the switch. But we couldn't outsmart our child. (He immediately declared the new Snuggly unacceptable.)

Snuggly has been out of our lives for about four decades. We got smarter with Jeremy and his "Gee" was a cloth diaper, easily replaced.

On Friday, I persuaded Seth who was visiting us for the holidays to go through some cartons under the eaves on our third floor as part of my never-ending effort to de-clutter our house. We found boxes with college books, and high school and camp memorabilia. Then, tucked in between copies of the college newspaper that Seth wrote a column for, I spotted Snuggly.

Memories of our little tyke franticly looking for Snuggly came rushing into my head. I didn't know whether to laugh or cry.

So I did both.

July 21, 2011

SON TIME

There are five very important males in my life: my husband Peter, our two sons, and our two grandsons. I never get enough time with any of them (except maybe Peter). But I especially miss our older son Seth who is the hardest to pin down because he's on the road or in his second home in Brazil.

So when we had him all to ourselves in New York City for forty-five hours last weekend, it was pure joy.

It didn't matter that we got to the Museum of Natural History too late to get tickets for its blockbuster exhibit on the brain, or that there were umbrella-breaking winds and torrential rain on Saturday. It didn't matter that there were no cabs as we made our way to Lincoln Center and therefore missed the first fifteen minutes of *War Horse*. Or that we had to walk through ankle-deep puddles to hail a cab.

What was important about the weekend was that we were part of his life. We ate at restaurants he likes and had coffee at a café where he writes. We rode his subway. We laughed through a play starring Chris Rock that has a word in the title that I don't feel comfortable writing. He was completely generous with his time.

My mother always asked me when I would be back again after my visits home. I understand how much it means to have a next visit on the calendar, and we don't have that. But this time, I left without my usual tears.

I was so grateful for my son time.

July 31, 2011

OUR CHILDREN ARE BETTER THAN WE ARE

In a recent blog entry, I mentioned writing a thank-you email to my primary care physician. That evening when Jeremy called, he told me that he had enjoyed that entry and added that he had recently sent a thank you card to his doctor.

Jeremy outdid me—he took the time to buy a card, put a stamp on it and take it to the mailbox. I like to think that he was brought up to do the right thing and now he does it better than I do. That got me to thinking about all the ways that our kids are better than we are.

I'm a decent writer and have published many travel articles over the years, just because I like to write. But Seth is a great writer and he actually makes a living as a journalist who writes a lot about travel. And honestly, I thought we were good parents. But both Peter and I think Jeremy and his wife Katrina are better at parenting than we were.

Exactly what we want—our children to be better than their parents.

October 27, 2011

OLDEN DAYS

When we visit the grandkids (Grady, age five, and Leo, almost eight), they always want to hear how things were in the olden days. Last weekend they were shocked to learn that their father hadn't started playing soccer until third grade, since they each started to play when they were two years old.

The kids also cannot conceive of life before email and had trouble believing that their dad didn't have email until he was in college. When a question came up that their 99-year-old great aunt could answer, Leo suggested we email her. "She doesn't do email," I told him. The look on his face was priceless. I explained that her hands were pretty arthritic and mostly used for knitting. When I added that she didn't even have a computer, his jaw dropped.

But it was their father who made the most startling observation. "Do you know, Mother," he said, "that on the day you were born the Civil War was as long ago as the day you were born is from today?"

It was then that I suggested we go outside and throw around the football.

March 22, 2012

Grandparents

I've been thinking about how lucky our grandsons are to have all four grandparents still living. My mother's mother passed away when I was two years old. Her husband who lived well into his nineties was the only grandparent in my life.

I never knew my father's parents and that didn't bother me until we became grandparents. If I knew their first names, and I don't think I did, I have forgotten them.

I decided to do some investigating. I called my older brother. He didn't know their names either. Then I tried Google.

I was surprised to see that my father and mother showed up—no details, no Facebook page, but a record of their existence. And for a fee, I might be able to learn more. However, I know a lot about my parents, so that was not necessary.

Without their first names, I couldn't find anything about my grandparents.

So I called Florence, my 95-year old half sister. She didn't remember when our father's parents died, but she knew that their names were Philip and Rebecca. She said Becky was an angel. She didn't say much about Grandpa Philip.

Our grandchildren won't have to search the Internet to learn about us. A couple of years ago, our son Jeremy asked us to write about our lives, which we did. He also videotaped us talking about our lives for our grandchildren to have after we are gone.

No such luck for me.

March 25, 2012

Bliss

Yesterday our baby turned forty.

Here is Jeremy at forty. Well-educated, good resume, great wife and children, good health and still a kid at heart. He has had some challenges but he has faced them with grace and wit.

This month he accepted a new job that suits him to a T. He is as happy as a pig in mud. When we talked yesterday, he was on his way to McDonalds to eat forty chicken McNuggets, keeping up a birthday tradition his parents would like to see end.

There is nothing a parent wants more than happy children.

August 9, 2012

Monterey, MA

Unless your kids are within an hour's drive (ours aren't), you never see them enough. We visit the grandchildren for a weekend every other month, and everyone comes to us for Thanksgiving. But this summer, we rented a house in the Berkshires and nabbed everyone for a week. The house was completely grandchildren-ready with toys and games galore, including air hockey,

Legos, all kinds of board games, a kayak and more.

We had great weather. We were a three-minute drive from a lake. We hiked and swam and went on nature walks. We picked blueberries from bushes we could reach from the deck. We watched about an hour of the Olympics each night. Our only disappointment was that Uncle Seth, flying back from St. Petersburg, Russia had a plane canceled and instead of having thirty-six hours with the family had only fifteen hours, including sleeping time.

Memorable moments: Eight-year-old Leo to his grandfather:" Gramps, your nose looks longer today." To his grandmother when asked his favorite subject in school: "Recess." Leo is all football, all the time, quizzing us about quarterbacks we've never heard of.

And Grady, in love with every caterpillar, Legos and entertaining us with typical five-year-old's jokes like What does one tomato say to the other? Answer: Ketchup with you later.

Driving home, I was sad. I thought I should be happy because I am so lucky to have had this week. But I was sad.

That is until we got home and Peter served me an extra- large dish of coffee ice cream.

August 12, 2012

FLORENCE AT CAMP

My (half-) sister Florence went to summer camp for two weeks. At age 95, she wasn't the oldest of the 100 campers. That title went to the 101 year-old-man who "power" walked every morning.

Peter and I were just an hour away, enjoying a week in the Berkshires. We had planned to visit Florence, and after failing to reach her by phone, we just showed up. It took us over an hour to find her because there were so many activities going on, but we caught up with her in the dining hall at lunchtime.

There she was in a navy Walker Art Museum sweatshirt, light slacks, and sneakers. She was having a great time, and was thrilled to see us. She told us about her busy camp days. She had attended an event the evening before where they played all the Academy-Award-winning songs since 1937 and she boasted that she knew all the words. But, she added sadly, "I can't remember what happened yesterday."

Florence is charming; she looks twenty years younger than she is. It was great to be with her. It made me wish that we had found each other much earlier in our lives.

As we got into the car, Florence said,

"You know, I don't refer to you as my half sister—you are my sister."

April 28, 2013

CHECKING IN WITH FLORENCE

When I checked in with Florence last week, she wasn't her usual upbeat self. Now ninety-six, she has just given up her car. "I failed the vision test," she explained. She also told me that her legs aren't working very well, so walking is a problem. She uses a "senior ride" service so that she can still go to the movies with friends, all of whom are younger than she is and used to depend on her for rides themselves.

But when Florence admitted that she is "finally feeling old", I was surprised. At seventy-five, I'm not feeling like a spring chicken myself. But if I can be like my half-sister, I have twenty-one more years to be young. I'll go with that.

December 26, 2013

MODEL FAMILY

On a billboard in Roraima, Brazil is an advertisement for CrediRapido, a loan company. It pictures a smiling family, the Kugels.

A Brazilian friend of Seth's was visiting her parents who live there last week, recognized Seth in the advertisement, and emailed him the photo. Seth posted it on Facebook with the following comment:

"If you're ever in Roraima, Brazil and need a loan, this company's spokesfamily seems incredibly trustworthy (not to mention good looking). Photo credit and sharp eye - Tammy Arnaud."

The photo in the ad was taken on our annual pre-Thanksgiving dinner walk two years ago. Somebody, somewhere, somehow snatched it from the Internet, having decided that we were a wholesome family, perfect for an advertisement. The irony is that Brazil is famous for its beautiful models, yet someone chose us! Of course, the price was right.

I doubt that it makes a difference, but they removed the football Peter was carrying, put leaves on the trees in the background and flipped the picture left to right. I am sure the perpetrators assumed that we would never see it.

Stay tuned to 70-Something.com for further developments. My post-retirement career as a model might be underway.

May 1, 2014

WEEKEND WITH A FIRE PIT

There were some noteworthy events at our regular visit to the grand-kids.

1. Being greeted at the school bus stop with a huge hug and a "Hi Grammy and Gramps!" from grandson Leo's friend Marcus. (Leo and his brother Grady hugged us too, but that's expected.)
2. Two flag-football games, a soccer game and a baseball game.
   However, perhaps the best moments of all were at Sunday night's cookout, followed by three generations sitting around the fire pit that

Jeremy built on one side of the house, roasting marshmallows for s'mores and singing around a blazing fire. It doesn't get any better than that.

June 5, 2014

College Reunion

Five years ago we went to Jeremy's fifteenth Amherst College Reunion to help take care of our grandchildren, then five and two.

On Saturday, we went to his twentieth reunion. This time, the grandchildren were so busy with other children that it took an offer of ice cream at Bart's to get time with them.

It was good to see them, even if only briefly, plus we got to hear Jeremy speak to his classmates as part of a panel on "How Did We End Up Where We Are 20 Years Later?" Jeremy talked about his startup that failed and the lessons he learned. He was poised, insightful and funny.

After the panel, we went to a buffet lunch for hundreds of reunion attendees. Once the grandkids were stuffed, they ran off with their friends. We stayed at our table and chatted with Jeremy's friends. We knew them all from the many parents' weekends. They are impressive 42-year-olds. Hearing about where they are in their lives, talking to them adult to adult was thrilling.

I couldn't resist passing Jeremy a napkin on which I had written "Thank you for sharing this with us."

June 26, 2014

Grammy and Gramps Camp

When our grandchildren Leo and Grady are out of school without scheduled activities, they go to "Mommy Camp", run seamlessly by our daughter-in-law. But when Katrina unexpectedly had to go to California for six days, she asked us to take over while Jeremy was at work.

We agreed, but I was concerned about having to drive the kids in Katrina's huge van around a town I didn't know. Also, at ages ten and almost eight, these boys are very active, and their play can get a little rough.

My goal was that Katrina would come home to no new scratches on either her car or her boys. I succeeded.

However, instead of being the perfect grandparents who come with gifts and can do no wrong, we were now the ones setting limits. Also we can't play soccer and do the other things that baby sitters do. But we drove them to swim practice; we bought them new bathing suits; we made trips to the grocery store.

We did the best we could, but the kids were always happy when Dad got home from work to play catch with them.

I explained to Grady and Leo, that although they might have more fun with other baby sitters, there aren't any babysitters that love them more than their grandparents.

July 17, 2014

AUNT RUTH @ 102

My visit to Aunt Ruth, who is 102, was overdue. Her kids told us that she's still amazing, but that there had been inevitable changes.

We decided to take an early morning flight to Buffalo, have lunch and a long afternoon with her and take an early evening bus to visit friends in Toronto for the weekend.

Recently, her children insisted that Aunt Ruth get a walker to get around her still elegant home, and they hired daytime help for her although she rages against the "all day" part. (The help is, of course, for *their* peace of mind.)

Aunt Ruth greeted us at the door. She was perfectly made up and elegantly dressed. She had a lunch of salmon and lentil salad delivered from the club she and my uncle belonged to for years, and everything was ready when we arrived. She would not allow us to lift a finger.

But the changes soon became apparent. Although she is completely "with it," her hearing has deteriorated, and we had to speak loudly and slowly. She told us that she can't taste anything any more so now she eats only because she knows she has to. She can read for fifteen minutes, and then she has to rest for twenty minutes. She is happy to be able to knit, and has sent more than 100 hats for homeless kids to Michigan where one of her sons lives.

We sat in the den after lunch and she wanted to hear everything about our kids, our grandchildren, and us. She spoke about the past and how hard it was to lose two husbands. But she still has her sense of humor, so when she opened a package from Macy's that contained two bottles of makeup, she laughed about whether, at her age, she should have only ordered one. Aunt Ruth had been a pillar of her community, serving on the boards of many non-profits. Now, she has only two friends from her past. One is 105 and one is turning 100. Her phone doesn't ring as much as it used to, (Note to self: call more often) and she doesn't get out much. On our last visit, she said she was tired and wanted to not wake up one morning, but she will live until her time is up.

It was hard for her when we left. I think her tears, were more about missing the past than for our going. She thanked us over and over again for coming.

September 25, 2014

The Last Visit of Summer

We visited the grandkids and their parents in Maryland last weekend. It was only a bit over two months since we last saw Leo (age 10) and Grady (almost 8), but they change fast. Here's the report.

Friday night: A football game at the private school where Jeremy is CFO.

Saturday morning: Grammy and Gramps split to attend simultaneous grandchildren's soccer games. Noted that both kids are taller than their teammates and that Leo's ten year old foot is bigger than his grandmother's.

Saturday afternoon: Road trip to Alexandria, VA. Walked the waterfront and King Street. Visited the art studios at The Torpedo Factory.

Sunday morning: The inevitable—grandson walks grandmother through the installation of a new operating system for her smartphone. Not so inevitable—grandson understood "spurious correlation."

Three generations discuss whether it's OK to do the crossword puzzle at a Starbucks using the shared newspaper provided. No agreement.

Sunday afternoon: Six boys, ages 4 to 42 play football on the front lawn, followed by a cookout with neighbors.

Monday Morning: Back home.

Summary: Grandkids grow too fast, know too much, live too far away.

October 12, 2014

Brazil Nut

When our children were little, I dreaded the first time they would cross the street alone. Keeping them safe was my highest priority and I thought only I could do that. Other milestones were just as scary: overnight camp, a driver's license, legal drinking age, and more.

But I never dreamed that one of our children would fall in love with Brazil, live in São Paulo for two years, go back whenever he could and, of this week, become a media star in that beautiful, yet complicated city 4,810 miles away from home.

So let me blatantly boast. He is about to appear on one of Brazil's top morning shows, having been written about in two of the country's leading newspapers and having had 48,577 hits in the first week of his new YouTube series "Amigo Gringo" – that helps Brazilians handle New York City challenges such as ordering bagels, using the subway, tipping and more. Trust me, the less than five-minute-long videos are funny. English subtitles require clicking on a box that says "cc" in the lower right hand corner of the screen.

Not quite what I expected of that little guy whose letters home during his first summer at overnight camp said they he had a stomach ache every day.

October 26, 2014

The Apple King

Almost three years ago, when our son Jeremy told us that he was going to eat an apple a day for 1000 days, we weren't surprised. He is, after all, our child who ate 40 Chicken McNuggets for his 40th birthday and later completed a "Meatless September" (a huge sacrifice for our meat-loving son) to raise money for charity.

At least apples are healthy.

Tomorrow he will eat his 1000th. He did not miss a day. Not even when he was in Guatemala over the summer. Or when he discovered late one night that there was not an apple in the house and had to run to the grocery store.

When the U.S. Apple Association learned (admittedly from Jeremy's mother who wanted to have a certificate made to mark his success), they were very excited to hear that this would come to "fruition" during National Apple Month. So they put him on their website.

And they sent him some apples.

March 15, 2015

White Castle Wackiness

Jeremy, our younger son and father of our two grandsons, successfully completed his eat-an-apple-a-day-for-a-1000-days marathon last October. Never content to be challenge-free, he decided to eat in the 100 highest revenue restaurant/fast-food chains in the U.S. in 1000 days. No one agreed to join him, but a friend's wife did pledge *not* to eat in any of those restaurants for the next 1000 days.

His parents rolled their eyes with that "here we go again" look.

On the Saturday of our NYC birthday celebration for Peter, Jeremy was in the living room of our Airbnb apartment when I woke up. He couldn't wait to tell me that he had discovered a restaurant on his list that was a three-minute walk away.

That's why I found myself, face unwashed, teeth unbrushed, in a White Castle restaurant at 7:00 a.m. The restaurant had been open all night. No one was there but us and the cook/server. Jeremy had a bacon, egg and cheese slider with a side of hash browns and a cherry coke. Needless to say, I had nothing. I think the total bill was $4.79.

What we do for our children!

June 11, 2015

PUPPY LOVE

After years of pleading, our grandchildren in Maryland got a "dog gift-certificate" for Xmas. They chose "Molly" at an animal shelter in early January. Her soulful eyes won their unanimous affection. I, a dog lover without a dog, was thrilled for them and couldn't wait to meet her.

Instead of sending us videos of our human grandchildren, Katrina and Jeremy sent us videos of Molly. Except for eating one of Jeremy's shoes, she made an easy transition into the family, but particularly bonded with the only other female in the house--Katrina. That creates an ongoing problem because each time Katrina leaves Molly goes to the window and whines.

When Peter and I met her on a March visit, Molly and I bonded too. She joined us when Jeremy drove us to the airport, and he reported that she whined at the window when we left the car.

According to Jeremy, when Molly heard my voice on speakerphone the other day, she licked it.

June 25, 2015

LIFE ISN'T FAIR

Sixteen years ago, I discovered a half-sister twenty-one years older than I am. When my father married my mother in 1930, he was divorced. In those days, people didn't talk bout divorce and so I never knew about his previous marriage.

In addition to a new sister, I gained a half-nephew, Paul and a half-niece Amy, who has two grown children. It's hard to make up for lost time, but we've tried. My sister, now 98, is doing well.

My niece Amy's son is 37, the father of two pre-school kids. Six weeks ago, he was diagnosed with colon cancer that has spread to his stomach. He is being treated, but it is a terminal disease. The median length of survival is two years.

His parents have come to spend the year in Boston while he is being treated and so we are seeing them as often as we can. It is unbearably sad.

July 2, 2015

The Diaper Pail

On Saturday, I threw away the tall white plastic container that sat in the basement next to our clothes dryer. Forty-five years ago it was a shiny new diaper pail. But because plastic never dies, it has stayed with us. Once we stopped using it for its original purpose, it became the default receptacle for dryer lint, fabric softener paper and other basement-generated garbage.

Because we upgraded our bedroom wicker laundry basket on Saturday, we replaced the diaper pail with our old one. Between our two boys, that pail probably held around 50,000 dirty diapers, give or take a few thousand.

When I dropped it into our recycling bin, I didn't think about those dirty diapers.

I wondered how two baby boys became grown ups so fast.

July 26, 2015

It's All Relative (s)

My mother's five siblings all lived in Buffalo, New York where she was born. When I was little, we visited there from Pittsburgh every summer. I was the only female in my generation, but I loved hanging out with my male cousins. I still do.

One of them, cousin Gerry, was unlucky in love until he met a beautiful widow named Kathryn at a college alumni gathering two years ago. She made her family debut at Gerry's son's wedding shortly thereafter, to rave reviews.

Kathryn has a cottage on tiny Clam Island, a five-minute motorboat ride from Branford, Connecticut. She and Gerry invited us to stop there for lunch on our way home from our road trip to take care of our grandchildren.

Talk about paradise. The island has no electricity, so evenings are early to bed or by candlelight after watching extraordinary sunsets. There are only seven houses on the island, and everybody seems to like everyone else. There is no 7-11 store so *everything* has to be carried in. Butane gas runs the refrigerator and the stove. The huge porch looks out over the rocks at Long Island Sound.

Kathryn made a stunning feast for a late lunch *al fresco* at a table set out on the rocks overlooking the water. Our cousins Joanie and Arnie joined us from Rhode Island. It was a scene straight out of *La Dolce Vita*.

Good news for Gerry—and the rest of the family.

September 3, 2015

My Nail Polish Chair

It was a Sunday night ritual. Peter, the kids and I would gather in our family room to watch TV or just "chill out" before the start of a new week. And I would polish my fingernails a fire-engine red that matched my lipstick.

I always sat in the big brown swivel lounge chair. I think the fabric was velour, but it is so worn now that I can't be sure.

When we sold the house the kids grew up in, the chair was relegated to the guest room of our current home. It's used mostly to hold just ironed-but-not-hung-up-yet clothing.

The other night I offered it to my half-niece and her husband who have moved here for a year while their grown son is treated for cancer at a Boston hospital. They are equipping the temporary home they have rented to be near him with second-hand furniture, and I thought they could use it. They agreed gratefully, and soon our 40-year-old chair will move to a new home.

I feel a bit sad about saying good-bye to my nail-polish chair.

October 4, 2015

Four Goalies

When we visit our grandsons in Maryland, we go to their soccer games. No longer little kids, both boys have become pretty good players.

And they are both goalies. Their father and his brother were goalies too. A powerful tradition.

We spent Saturday afternoon on the soccer field at the school where their dad works with our two former goalie sons and our two goalie grandsons trying to score against each other.

Seeing both of my sons in goal (How many years since that has happened?) trading shots against each other and my grandsons…is that a grandmother moment, or what?

On Sunday, we had to decide which kid's game to attend or spend six hours (three of which were travel) to see both. You can't have a favorite grandson—so we went to two games. We drove 137 miles, almost the entire Virginia/Maryland beltway to see both boys' teams lose.

Who cares that they didn't win?

October 18, 2015

Ich Bin Ein Berliner

Last Monday, our son Jeremy and his sons became German citizens in a ceremony at the German embassy in Washington, DC.

This was possible because Article 116 of Germany's constitution permits those who had their citizenship revoked for "political, racist, or religious reasons" during the Nazi regime to reapply for German citizenship while retaining their current citizenship.

Decades ago, my husband Peter's family was stripped of their German citizenship after they fled from Berlin to escape the Nazis. He was six. Now Germany welcomes back Peter and his descendants.

In a moving ceremony, the Counsul General apologized for "a terrible chapter in German history." He thanked the new citizens for their "act of faith that Germany has changed."

Our daughter-in-law Katrina wrote on her Facebook page: "In the 1930s, Peter Kugel and family were stripped of their German citizenship. Today his son and grandsons became German citizens…Take that, Hitler."

November 1, 2015

MOTHER VS. SON

In my fifties and sixties, I published dozens of travel articles in *The Boston Globe* and other publications. True, I did not write nearly as many as our son Seth writes as *The New York Times'* Frugal Traveler, and they weren't as good (except for "Mother and Son on Safari" which we wrote jointly for the *Globe)*. Nonetheless, he was *not* the first travel writer in the family.

Anyhow, seven years ago, I started this blog which is more fun than travel writing.

A year ago, Seth started a YouTube channel, Amigo Gringo, that gives Brazilians (and others) tips about navigating New York City. Many thousands view his twice-weekly videos. He gets stopped on the streets of New York or Rio or São Paulo by people who recognize him from the videos or his TV guest appearances.

I, on the other hand, get stopped by strangers in grocery stores who ask, "Aren't you Judy Kugel? I recognize you from your blog."

But it's not a mother versus son contest. Or is it?

January 7, 2016

THE SNOW MAN

Between Christmas and New Year's, we had an unexpected visit from Seth. Although he came to see a good friend of his who was in town from California, his visit was our good luck.

The first morning he was here, he was a special guest on Minnesota Public Radio News for a one-hour discussion on travel "bucket lists" via Skype. How odd it was to be sitting in our dining room streaming

Minnesota Public Radio live on my computer and listening to Seth who was on the air chatting with the host in Minnesota, but talking from his bedroom in Cambridge just above us. The wonders of technology…

Boston had its first snow of the unseasonably warm winter the night he arrived. More good luck, he shoveled for us in the afternoon, no technology involved…

May 8, 2016

ON BEING A MOTHER

Forty-six years into it, I'm still working on being a good mother. I've had a lot of jobs over my (blessedly) long life, but being a mother is the hardest. It's also the most important.

Here are some of the lessons I have learned:

1. There is no perfect mother.
2. There is no perfect child.
3. You can still aspire to being either (1) or (2).
4. Have important (but easy) rules while they grow up, like:
   a. Two cookies at lunch; three cookies at dinner.
   b. Soft drinks only on the weekends (except at friends' houses)
   c. Limited TV on school nights. (If my children were young now, it would be "No phones at the dinner table and no phones in the bedroom overnight.")
5. "Ask your father." doesn't work.
6. Two serious sports a year is enough.

And once they are grown up:

1. Don't call them. Wait for them to call you.
2. Unconditionally love whoever loves them.
3. Be careful what you ask.
4. Manage your expectations.

If you are lucky you will eventually be rewarded with grandchildren. They're a lot easier.

June 2, 2016

PARTY RULES

It's been a long time since we gave birthday parties for our children. And the rules have changed.

The pediatric wisdom in the 1970's limited the guest list to the age of the child plus one. For those who are math challenged that would be six kids for the fifth birthday. Nowadays, if you don't invite everyone in the class or play group, you are in trouble with the party cops.

Back then kids played games like Pin the Tail on the Donkey. At the most exotic parties, there would be a clown or a magician. I recall Seth in cape and high hat playing the magician's role at his brother's fourth birthday party. Now there are bouncy tents, visits to indoor pool complexes and I don't know what else.

So, imagine my trepidation when I decided to give a birthday party for Seth and his two best high school friends the other night. One friend was in town from California, one lives here and Seth was visiting from New York.

I decided to forego the party favors. We did have candles, but only the two gracing our dinner table. Instead of kid-fare, I made a dinner party as if I were entertaining President Obama. Wine flowed. Conversation was of the grownup variety.

But still, it was our kid, his friends and a birthday party.

June 26, 2016

BEST FATHER'S DAY GIFT EVER

When Seth was home in May, he remarked on his father's dreadful posture as he worked on his laptop computer. I told Seth that I'd stopped nagging Peter about it because it just makes him angry at me.

But Seth had a solution. For Father's Day, he and Jeremy would get Peter a large monitor that he would have to sit up straight to see.

It took three separate deliveries—the monitor, the wireless keyboard and the wireless track-pad. For once, Peter's lack of attention paid off and I managed to get all three parts into the house without his noticing.

Example: Me: "Honey, was that the doorbell?" Peter: "No". Me: "Well I'd better check. Nope, it was nothing," I said as I walked by our study carrying a huge package.

When Peter opened Seth's Father's Day card that Friday, it mentioned the gift without revealing what it was, but it said that he expected it to be in use by the time he called on Sunday. So I decided to give it to Peter early.

I have known my husband for fifty-one years. I have never seen him cry. But his reaction to this thoughtful, caring gift from his children looked a lot like tears were going to appear. I said, "If you were a crier, would you be crying now?"

He nodded.

July 31/16

MY HALF-FAMILY

Except for our cousins Judy and Steve who moved away in 1975, I've not had family members living nearby for more than 40 years. This year, I have seven.

It started when my half-sister's grandson Jonathan moved here a year ago from New Orleans for cancer treatment. His parents (my half-niece Amy and her husband Ken) moved to Boston from Minnesota to help him and his young family. They too have now been here a year. And then in January, my half-sister Florence, age 99, moved here to be near her daughter Amy.

Last Sunday, everybody came to our house for lunch. Even Jonathan's mother-in-law joined us. Our guests' ages ranged from three to ninety-nine. Four generations, all related to me.

Florence, at 99, has trouble hearing, even when she's wearing her hearing aids and she needs a walker. Elliot at three is a ball of energy. His brother Adam, at five is never without a book.

But food is a great age equalizer, and we had plenty of that. Even better, we played *Wits and Wagers*, a marvelous game for all ages. Except for some sofa pillows out of place, our home was none the worse for wear when everybody left at four o'clock.

My half-family is here for a sad reason. But we still have fun together, and that is gratifying.

August 25, 2016

EIGHT DAYS IN AUGUST

It started on a Friday morning when cousin Gerry and his son arrived from Connecticut for a weekend of Boston Red Sox games. Our daughter-in-law Katrina arrived from Maryland late that afternoon, having dropped her husband Jeremy and brother-in-law Seth off in Western Massachusetts for Camp Becket's Dad's Weekend. On Sunday, we drove a round-trip to Becket to spend an hour or so with our grandsons just as I had thirty-some years ago when Seth and Jeremy were campers there.

Jeremy, Katrina and Seth came back here for the week between Dad's Weekend and the end of camp rather than drive back and forth to Maryland again. Gerry and son had left while we were away. (A good thing because we needed their beds!)

Tuesday, we all drove to Cape Cod for a reunion with former neighbors, Seth, Peter and me just for the day, but Jeremy and Katrina to stay on the Cape for two days. Everyone was back here for dinner on Thursday night. On Friday, the kids left—Seth to go back to New York, Jeremy and Katrina to pick up the boys at camp.

From chaos to quiet...

That is until the next day when friends from California arrived. Needless to say, we were exhausted from all this fun. So was our washing machine.

It died during the third load of sheets and towels.

August 26, 2016

LEO'S VOICE

When our Seth wrote an article about kids planning their family vacations, he offered his nephew (our grandson) Leo as an example.

Leo, age twelve, had planned a school vacation trip in March for his younger brother Grady, his parents, his grandmother (yours truly) and his Aunt Nancy. He chose the destination (New Orleans), the hotel and most of the activities.

Shortly after Seth's article appeared, National Public Radio (NPR) asked if they could interview Leo for *Morning Edition*. Leo, away at summer camp, agreed. The phone interview took place in the camp's business office during "siesta".

It aired last Saturday morning and for 3:05 minutes, we heard our twelve-year-old grandson answering questions from Scott Simon, host of *Morning Edition*. Leo was articulate and funny and he didn't sound nervous (although he said he was).

His mother listened to it "live" at home, then "live" in Chicago and finally "live" in San Francisco on her smartphone. His grandmother downloaded it to her computer and has listened countless times.

It was fun to hear from several friends and colleagues who were listening to Morning Edition and just happened to hear our grandson being interviewed.

There is one person, however, who has refused to listen. His name is Leo.

October 27, 2016

The Visit

We all want to be better parents than our parents. We may succeed in small ways, but there is no such thing as perfect parents.

For example, my parents always tried to pin me down about my next trip home as I left after a visit. But however much I loved them, in my busy life, it wasn't so easy to just get on a plane home.

Remembering those moments, I try not to ask our departing children how soon they will be back.

So imagine my surprise and delight when Seth found a few open days in his calendar and decided he could "work" at "home." He arrived by bus on Sunday afternoon, and within an hour we were off to dinner and the theater, having been able to get an extra ticket for him.

The next morning, he commandeered the dining room table and wrote all day. He would take a break now and then, and luckily I was here to take advantage of every second. Tuesday was more of the same and Wednesday morning at 9:00 a.m., he was gone.

What he got from his visit: the company of his loving parents, some quiet time to write, theater and dinner out and a refrigerator full of his favorite food. In addition, he left with my extra set of iPhone earbuds and half of our remaining supply of his favorite cheese.

It was a win-win visit.

November 13, 2016

CELEBRATING AUNT RUTH

My mother grew up in Buffalo, New York and her five brothers and sisters never left. So I have visited my family there countless times. When I was a child, my mother and I often spent summers in my Aunt Ruth's house in Buffalo with my three male cousins and my beloved Uncle Milton.

But Friday's visit was different because it was the day of Aunt Ruth's memorial service, and it marked the end of an era.

She had been a much-loved member of the Buffalo community. When she turned 100, the non-profit boards she served on refused to accept her resignation. She passed a driver's "re-test" with flying colors in her late nineties which allowed her to keep driving her younger friends who were "too old to drive" everywhere. At age 104, you don't have many peers, but she had so many younger friends that she never lacked visitors or calls as she grew frail.

In his memorial speech, her eldest son, Ken, told of the time she called the summer camp director after she heard that he had announced over the loud speaker that her son needed to move to the "overweight" table, humiliating him in public. The camp director never did that again. "Woe to the person who brought ketchup or mustard to the table in a bottle," reported Ken because everything had to be just so in her house. He admitted that that person had usually been him.

At 104, she was tired and ready to "go" and decided to refuse food and water. But soon, Ken said, she "got hungry".

Aunt Ruth was one of a kind—beautiful, gracious, and generous. Now she is gone. I will never stop missing her.

December 4, 2016

LOSING JONATHAN

KAMINSKY, Jonathan Edward Age 38, of Arlington, formerly of New Orleans, Olympia, Seattle, Palau, Berkeley, Brooklyn, Madagascar, Minneapolis/St. Paul, and Sweden, on Sunday, November 27, 2016. Journalist, athlete, singer and writer of songs. He is survived by his wife Sarah, sons Adam & Elliot, parents Amy & Ken, brother David, grandmother Florence, and many loving friends.

There is nothing sadder than parents outliving their children. My cousins Amy and Ken moved half-way across the country to be with their son Jonathan during his eighteen months of colon-cancer treatment in Boston and they were here for him and his family every moment of what turned out to be an incurable illness.

Jonathan's memorial service on Thursday honored his wish that it be a celebration. His friends fought back tears as they spoke. But they also made us laugh with tales of Jonathan's charming and quirky behavior, his love of music and bad jokes and of course his devotion to Sarah and Adam and Elliot. The ceremony ended with one of his close friends fulfilling Jonathan's wish to play, "So Long, It's Been Good to Know Ya..." on his guitar. We all joined in.

It felt like Jonathan was there with us.

December 16, 2016

CELEBRATING FLORENCE

It isn't every day that your half-sister turns 100. It's especially special when you've only known her since she was 82.

That's why Sunday, on Florence's birthday, I was happy to host her centennial party. Everyone there (except for her great-grandchildren, ages three and five) knew her far longer than I did.

The party theme was "Queen for a Day." Her "jeweled crown was created by our across-the-street neighbor's seven-year-old who also supplied a boa and cape. Cards and calls came from all across the country.

Florence doesn't hear too well, and she uses a walker. She has endured the loss of a son and a grandson. Yet her sense of humor is in excellent working condition and people want to be with her. She loved being the center of attention.

January 1, 2017

ANOSMIA

Our favorite guest blogger (Peter Kugel) kicks off 2017…

At 86, I've reached the age at which, as the lyrics of September Song put it, "the days dwindle down to a precious few." And the days aren't the only things that are dwindling down.

Judy recently asked me if I was enjoying the aroma her cooking was producing in the kitchen and I reminded her that I have pretty much lost my sense of smell. She asked me if I missed it. Somewhat to my surprise, I realized that I didn't and I wondered why.

Smells are important. I remember what may have been the best breakfast I ever had. It was at a non-descript hotel in Oslo. It featured a variety of breads that had just come out of the oven and they had a smell that only fresh-baked bread has. The cheese and butter that were served with them also had memorable smells that the cheese and butter we get from the supermarket don't, with subtle overtones like those that summer tomatoes used to have until they discovered how to make tomatoes out of cardboard.

Those smells, and many others, are lost to me now. But I realize that they were mostly lost to me when I was younger because I didn't pay them much attention. Now that I don't have all that many breakfasts left, I pay more attention. Although my breakfasts feature ordinary toast and ordinary butter, that I couldn't smell even if they were special, I enjoy them more.

Gold isn't precious because it's wonderful. Iron is stronger. Aluminum is lighter. It's precious because there isn't much of it.

Perhaps that's why they call them "the golden years".

January 15, 2017

Hanging Out

It isn't that I don't want to be with old folks. After all, I am one. But kids are just more fun.

Recently, we and our kids and grandkids were invited to dinner at their neighbors. Tess, the neighbors' daughter, a junior in high school, was leaving for three months in Costa Rica and this was her goodbye dinner. Her sister Emily is a freshman in college. Since we have only boys--sons and grandsons--we love hanging out with Tess, Emily and their parents when we go to Maryland.

That evening their mother had to make a meal that fit the needs of her vegan husband, a vegetarian daughter, two gluten-free guests, and our son Jeremy who during the month of January isn't eating anything beginning with the letter "e". (Don't ask.)

Not that I am trying to brag, but when you hang out with kids, you learn some cool stuff.

Before dinner got going, we set up a group on WhatsApp to keep up with Tess in Costa Rica. Next, they helped me make a set of personalized emojis. For those as clueless as I was, those are avatars that you customize to look like yourself. You can choose from hundreds of possibilities to enhance whatever you are saying in a text or email.

After a feast of a dinner that (miraculously) had something for everyone, the ten of us played a card game called "Pig". It is probably the silliest game I've ever played. We laughed all the way through it.

Nobody mentioned aches or pains.

January 19, 2017

Take Your Parents to Work Day

Our son Jeremy is the chief financial officer of a private boys school. We've seen the school and its beautiful campus (overseeing it is one of his responsibilities) when there were no students on campus, but on Friday, school was in full swing on "Take Your Parents to Work Day". We were the sole participants.

As we walked up the stairs to his office, we saw lots of flyers with pictures of us on the wall:

> "Warning: If you see the two characters pictured above
> here on campus, call security immediately!!"

Jeremy introduced us to his colleagues and we all headed to the cafeteria for a bountiful lunch with hundreds of jacket-and-tie-clad noisy boys and their teachers.

Jeremy's staff had a few question for us. Among other things, they wanted to know what kind of a child he was (great) and how he got to be so funny (inherited from his father).

A trip to the school store to buy his father a sweatshirt and we were on our way.

2

IN IT FOR THE LONG HAUL

MARRIAGE

"A happy marriage is the union of two good forgivers."
Robert Quillen

I was thirty when Peter and I married three years after we met. Pretty late for my generation, but right for me. Our solid marriage, our deep friendship, our pride in our family, and our good fortune are at least partially a result of our timing.

When people ask us what we attribute our successful marriage to, we reply, "No one else would have us." In reality, part of it is luck. We've both been gainfully employed and although not super-rich, we've haven't had the financial worries that plague so many young people today. We've both had successful careers. We had no huge college loans ourselves, and relative to now, college was affordable for our children. We drive low-end cars and don't spend a lot on entertainment. Travel has been our splurge.

Peter is a true intellectual, and I manage to hold my own in that department. He's the thinker, and I'm the talker. We both love classical music and although I could like today's popular music, I'm OK without it. We both like to cook, but since he doesn't see dirt, I usually clean up. And I'm OK with that too.

We have similar taste in movies, in paint colors and in food (except for his dislike of red peppers and olives). Even though I can't eat gluten, I usually quietly accept his breakfast choices of all the things I can't have. I have been known to take longer to get over our few disagreements, and he is OK with that.

Is that a formula for success to be emulated? No idea. It works for us.

Marriage is a journey. Luckily, for us it has been an easy trip. On the rare occasion when I am not adoring my husband, I think of love advice columnist Ann Lander's wonderful response to wives who are questioning their marriages.

"Are you better off with him or without him?" Not an issue for me.

January 24, 2008

BICKERING

Call it squabbling; call it minor arguments, call it what you will. My husband Peter and I bicker. Inevitably, it's about something ridiculous.

For example, this morning I asked Peter why he was mailing a letter to a person in a place he was actually going to be within the next two hours. If he carried it by hand, a) it would get there sooner, and b) it would save a stamp.

"Oh," he replied, "I'm going to the gym first, and I don't want to carry the letter with me."

I retorted, "That's really stupid!"

This "conversation" took place between two people who totally love each other and have for more than 40 years. Two people who have a great marriage. Two people who hardly ever argue about anything important, at least not since the kids left home. So I wonder, does every couple bicker?

One of our sons called attention to our bickering from the back seat of our car when we were lost. It wasn't all that long ago. We were stunned. We had never noticed it before. But, of course, he was right.

Cars are a great location for bickering, especially if one member of the couple has no sense of direction, and the other won't ask for directions. Sound familiar? Or for a car parking example:

"You're a mile from the curb."

"No I'm not. I'm directly behind the car parked in front of us."

I wouldn't want to give the impression that bickering occupies a disproportionate amount of our time. Most of the time, we are best friends, always appreciating each other, always helping each other.

But still, we bicker.

February 29, 2008

Leap Year

Forty years ago today, on a chairlift in Cortina, Italy I asked Peter to marry me and he said "no". Back then, February 29th was the only day women could ask men to dance (or marry). But then women didn't going skiing in Europe with their boyfriends either.

I remember finding a letter addressed to me from my mother on the hall table in our chalet. She would not have been happy to know that I was registered with my "married" name. Of course, the owner had no idea that I was the intended recipient of the letter since there was no one with my name staying there.

Peter didn't actually say "no" that day. He said, "When it's time to ask, I'll do the asking." Since we were high on a chair lift in Italy, I couldn't exactly get up and storm out of the relationship. Which was lucky because four months later he did ask, and forty years later, I can say it was worth waiting.

March 10, 2008

Peter's Birthday

Today is Peter's birthday. This is not a birthday that is divisible by five or ten. Yet it seems to be very important, and I am asking myself why. At 78, he is still handsome and smart and my best friend.

I think this birthday is important because in spite of his good health and our good luck, we only have so many years left together, and we are both becoming more aware of that. When I married an "older" man (although only by eight years), I never considered that eventually, our age difference might become important. And even if I had considered that, I would have reminded myself that I would be grateful for any years that we might have together.

Or maybe it has something to do with my being 70 now. Because even though Peter thinks I am beautiful, smart and his best friend, I'm not the woman I used to be. In some ways, I think I'm better. And in some ways, together we are better than ever.

March 8, 2008

HAYDN'S 88TH SYMPHONY

Several bars from Haydn's 88th Symphony are engraved on the inside of my wedding band. There's no "to my darling on our wedding day," no set of our initials, no date of our marriage. Just the first several bars of the last movement of Haydn's 88th Symphony.

When we were dating, Peter had found it amusing that my college friends and I learned to identify symphonies for music class exams by putting words to the tunes. "Eat pretzels, drink beer cause Haydn is here" comes to mind as does "Mozart's in the closet—let him out, let him out, let him out".

So when we were contemplating getting engaged, (actually I was contemplating it more than he was) we put some words to the theme of the last movement of Haydn's 88th symphony. "I am going to Mr. Gusil's, I am going to Mr. Gusil's," Mr. Gusil was a jewelry designer whose shop we frequently passed and who I hoped would design my engagement ring some day.

We did, of course, get engaged and the engagement ring came from Mr. Gusil's. But it was only on our wedding day that I found the engraved music inside my wedding ring.

Last night, almost 40 years later, we attended a concert of the Handel and Haydn Society. The program included Haydn's 88th Symphony. I don't think we had ever heard it live before. When the theme of the fourth movement filled the hall, I grabbed Peter's hand, and my eyes filled with tears.

They were playing our song.

May 1, 2008

OLDER MEN

The man I have loved for 43 years is eight years older than I am. I have a vivid memory of seeing him for the first time. There was no way to get to my new job by public transportation back in 1965, and my first car, a red VW bug, hadn't arrived at the car dealer on time. My new employer arranged for me to be picked up at a subway stop, and my ride to work (believe it or not in his red VW bug) was with Peter. Of course I remember what I was wearing that July day, and I remember his light blue sports jacket. I had no idea if he was single. (He was.)

Three years later, we were married. By then, we didn't work at the same place, and I can remember coming home from work day after day with butterflies of excitement in my stomach at the thought of seeing him. It was like being excited about a date every day. I never gave a thought to his being eight years older.

But things are a bit different now that I have turned 70 and he is 78. Although he is pretty healthy, the odds are strong that I will outlive him. He's always been an absent-minded professor, but now he seems a bit more forgetful. He claims to have less energy. We do worry about each other more now, and I often wish that he too were 70.

Now he is usually home before me, and when I open the door and I hear his "Hi honey!" my first response is relief, knowing that he is fine. Then I feel the butterflies.

March 12, 2009

MY BELOVED AT SEVENTY-NINE

My beloved husband turned seventy-nine this week. It seemed to me like we just celebrated his seventy-eighth birthday. He'll be eighty before we know it. How do we slow down time?

In school, I was one of the youngest children in my grade. When all my classmates were driving, and I had months to go until my sixteenth birthday, the days and weeks seemed to drag on and on. Now the weeks and months are flying. How do we make the most of the unknown number of days we have left together?

One of the amazing things about Peter is his attitude. He has lived longer than both of his parents; he has glaucoma (good for me because he still thinks I am beautiful) and a year ago he got a hearing aid. He doesn't like not standing in front of a college class, which he did for thirty-some years. So now he teaches in an institute for retirement learning. And he only teaches things he doesn't know so he can learn along with his "students." He goes to the gym every day. Unlike his wife, he is not a complainer.

He is as interesting today as he was the day I met him, and I am grateful for every moment that we are together.

October 1, 2009

P.D.

It has taken me a year to be able to write that Peter, my husband and best friend, has Parkinson's Disease. For some time he had been experiencing fatigue and having other issues that could be, and often are, symptoms of aging. He had seen his primary care doctor and a geriatrician, but they were unable to come up with an explanation. It took a retired doctor whom Peter barely knew to suggest Parkinson's Disease.

In June of last year, Peter went on a bike ride with some friends. At a lunch three months later, Peter sat next to the retired doctor who had been on that bike ride. He asked Peter if he could tell him something that he (Peter) might not like to hear. Peter agreed. The doctor told him that he had noticed on that early summer bike ride that, while off his bike, Peter walked in a gait that suggested Parkinson's Disease. When Peter got home, he Googled Parkinson's Disease and then sent me an email at work saying "I think I know what's wrong with me."

Weeks later, he saw a neurologist. There is no actual test for Parkinson's Disease, but responding to Sinamet, a drug that replaces what is not produced by the brain of people with PD, is a good indicator of the disease.

The good news was that the wondering about what was going on was over. The bad news was that we were faced with a serious disease that has a lot of uncertainty related to it. We had no idea about how the disease would progress. Would Peter's quality of life change significantly? Would we need to move out of our house? Would we have to curtail our active lifestyle?

There is no answer that works for everyone, but everyone wants an answer.

More good news is that Peter is coping well. The Sinamet has helped. Peter does not complain. We have learned a lot about the disease in the past year. And we have learned to accept some of our limitations and to be grateful for what we can do.

Peter used to remind me that we never say, "I'm fortunate because my big toe is not hurting today."

Well, my big toe doesn't hurt today.

August 9, 2009

FOR BETTER OR FOR WORSE, BUT NOT FOR LUNCH

It was my husband Peter who recently reminded me of that wise saying. Although I am not ready to retire, it's bound to happen eventually. And when it does, who knows how often we'll both be home at lunchtime. I know that I will be busy doing things I don't have time for now, but do I want to be hanging around with Peter more?

He and I have had a marvelous marriage for forty-one years and ten days. Peter has been retired for four years and, although he misses teaching, he has filled his time with activities that suit him, but don't always take him out of the house for lunch.

My friend Susie and her husband, both retired, seem to manage being together very well. For years, they worked together in their business. For some couples, that would be the kiss of death. But they both have a great sense of humor, an active social and community life, and grandchildren to dote on. It sounds as though they never get too much of one another.

So the other night, I asked Susie how they managed to pull off this 24/7-together-thing so well. She explained by telling me about her day. She was on her way out to do some errands. Her husband said, "I'll come with you." "OH NO YOU WON'T!" replied Susie.

Sounds right to me.

August 20, 2009

My Favorite Five Minutes

It surprises me to see little kids without jackets when I am bundled up to keep warm outside. Trouble staying warm is another one of the increasing number of growing-older symptoms that I've encountered since turning seventy.

So it comes as no surprise that when Peter and I go to bed at this time of the year, there are four ice-cold hands under the covers. This does not encourage us to rush into each other's arms.

That is why my favorite five minutes of the day are between 6:05 a.m. when our alarm goes off and 6:10 a.m. when I have to get out of bed. I turn off the alarm and reach over to the toasty-warm body lying next to me.

And for those five minutes, everything is right with the world.

December 5, 2010

Who Goes First?

The odds are that Peter and I will not die at the same time. Statistically, I should outlive him because I am eight years younger than he is. But life is not statistics.

Peter doesn't want to outlive me because he thinks I take care of him. A number of years ago, our son Seth offered to take Peter as a roommate should I die first, but I think that offer may have expired.

Which brings me to this morning. Normally, Peter folds his laundered socks and puts them away. But today, I did it. In his sock drawer, I found six "orphans". Turns out they all matched and he actually has three more pairs of socks. My thought was that one thing I wouldn't miss about Peter, should I outlive him, would be how badly he takes care of his clothes.

I decided to make a mental list of "at least I won't have to live with THAT anymore" things that might offer me some consolation in an unhoped-for widowhood.

I couldn't think of anything else.

August 4, 2011

DATE NIGHT

Although we often go out to dinner with friends, we don't usually go out to dinner by ourselves. We like to cook, and since we must choose restaurants carefully when we do go out because of my gluten intolerance, eating at home makes a lot of sense for us.

But our wedding anniversary is different. Last week we celebrated our forty-third. And we did it in style. I left work on time. We got dressed up. We went to one of our favorite restaurants. The waiter was great, the food was delicious. But the best was how much fun we had together.

I wish we could have forty-three more.

December 1, 2011

FRAIL

Recently, a couple of our friends have suggested that Peter is looking a bit frail. It's hard for me to notice any change because I am with him every day. But as I look a little closer, it seems that they may be right. After all, as our children remind me, "He's no spring chicken."

No matter, he is still the person I adore, and I am thankful for every day we have together.

As we held each other before drifting off to sleep the other night, I thought about how our bodies fit together so well, how comfortable they are together still and how we know every inch of one another as if we were one.

June 17, 2012

REWINDING THE TAPE

I came home Friday evening feeling a little stressed. The week at work had not seen my best performance as a manager, and I wasn't feeling so great about it. So since we don't have a cat to kick...

When I walked into the house, I saw that Peter had made a purchase that replaced something similar that he had never used. So, of course, I am thinking, "Why not get it right the first time?" What's more, he had bought it at a store where we get a 15% discount that he forgot to use. It was expensive enough so the discount would have mattered.

Considering that we had just spent a small fortune to paint the outside of our house and that someone wrecked our car's fender while it was parked yesterday without leaving a note, the added expense just hit me the wrong way. Let's put it like this, I could have started the weekend in a friendlier way.

I proceeded directly to the basement to lift weights. There, I thought about how inappropriate my reaction was. The thing Peter bought is really important to get right, and I should have said, "What a good idea!" Compared to the painter's bill and the expected cost of the car repair, the expense was practically nothing.

So when I finished my weights and came upstairs to find my wonderful husband making dinner, I asked him, "Can we rewind the tape?"

August 30, 2012

WRONG ANSWER

Our son Seth called us from Martha's Vineyard the other night. It was his first visit to that beautiful island off the coast of Massachusetts, and he found it quite terrific.

I told Seth that I had fallen in love with his father during a camping weekend with friends on Martha's Vineyard about forty-six summers ago. It had rained very hard the first night, and I recall that, once it stopped, we gathered around a campfire. Peter was putting his wet sneakers on a rock close to the flames to dry.

It was as if I was hit by a ton of bricks because I suddenly realized that I was in love with that man drying his sneakers. I don't know if it was watching him interact with his close friends, or what, that caused me to realize that he was the one for me.

Unfortunately, he was a little slower at falling in love with me, but the years have proved it was worth the wait.

After we finished our phone conversation with Seth, I asked Peter when he realized that he had fallen in love with me. "No idea, he said."

Wrong answer.

December 13, 2012

FOCUS

On our weekend walk, a guy zipped by us on his bicycle. Outfitted in blue and black Spandex, his bike was thin-wheeled and fast. I told Peter that I didn't think he noticed us.

Even if he did, he probably didn't imagine himself as one of an elderly couple like us who had once zipped along bike paths in Spandex or its earlier equivalent.

And that got us to arguing. Peter claimed that we focus mainly on people in our own age group and that is why he didn't notice us. Three-year olds look at other three-year olds; teenagers at teenagers and old folks at old folks.

No, I insisted. Every workday I focus on people in younger generations because no one at work is my age and that is what I like to do.

We then launched into full bickering mode, moving from where we focus our attention to what defines happiness and more. At one point we found something to agree on, but I forget what.

Our walk takes about forty minutes. Any longer and our marriage might have been in trouble.

January 2, 2013

80-SOMETHING GUEST APPEARANCE

Hi. I'm Judy's husband, Peter. Because I'm eight years older than she is, she invited me to tell you how things look to an eighty-something.

In your seventies, you're part of what gerontologists call the "young-old". Some time in your eighties you graduate and become one of the "old-old". Of course it happens at different times for different people, but it's starting to happen to me now. At eighty-two, I look like an old man and I walk like an old man. But I don't feel like an old man, so it startles me when pregnant women offer me their seats on the bus.

I take pills like an old man (seventeen a day). And when I wake up in the morning, I can appreciate the old joke about how if you wake up in the morning and nothing hurts, you're dead.

I think I hurt less than I might because (thanks in part to Judy's example) I stretch before breakfast and go to the gym during the day. I realize that aging is inevitable unless you avoid it by dying. But I am convinced that exercise makes it less bad, not only by slowing it down, but also by making you feel better when you do it.

When I walk or bike, almost everyone else passes me. In the olden days, when we went on biking vacations, I was at the head of the pack. Now, the pack has to wait for me. I used to run marathons. Now, I can hardly run at all. I make lists to help me remember what I want to do, but I forget where I put the lists. Almost everything I do takes longer and I don't do it as well as I used to.

What surprises me is that it doesn't make me unhappy. Recent research into happiness suggests why.

Happiness seems to be a relative thing. Like perception. A flashlight that doesn't look like much during the day can look quite bright at night. And happiness researcher Daniel Kahneman suggests a way to demonstrate that relativity. Fill three bowls with water, one lukewarm, one a bit cooler and the third a bit warmer. Put one hand in the cooler bowl and one in the warmer. Leave them there for a minute and then put them both into the lukewarm bowl. It will feel cold to the hand that was in the warm bowl and warm to the one that was in the cool bowl. Same bowl.

Different perceptions.

Fortunately, happiness seems to work pretty much the same way. Although doing things as slowly and badly as I do in my eighties would have depressed me in my forties, it doesn't depress me today. I still enjoy learning new things, working on new projects, drinking martinis, eating chocolate, listening to Mozart, seeing my grandchildren and going to bed with Judy.

As Chekov put it: "Even in Siberia, there is happiness."

May 22, 2013

SATURDAY MORNING

Peter was reading the newspaper when I came downstairs on Saturday morning. He did manage to look up and say "Good morning." He was sipping a cup of freshly brewed coffee. He looked quite content.

While he read, I sorted the laundry and started the first load, watered the plants, gathered piles of winter clothes and coats to take to the cleaners and straightened up a bit from our dinner guests the night before.

Then I had some toast and coffee with him.

When I was cleaning up from breakfast, I noticed that there was a lot of water puddled on the stovetop. To mop it up, I had to remove the grates and the trays under the burners and make several trips to the sink with dripping sponges.

Now, I don't mind doing the laundry, watering the plants etc. while Peter reads the paper. But there was something about all that water that got to me. So I said in my most obnoxious voice—"I don't mind doing the laundry and watering the plants and getting the cleaning ready while you sit with the paper and your coffee, but don't you think you could have at least cleaned up the water on the stove when the tea kettle boiled over?"

Even our almost-perfect forty-five year marriage has it bad moments. But I immediately regretted speaking angrily to the man who bakes me great gluten-free bread, mows the lawn, listens to my endless stories about work and gave me two great sons.

I decided that I should have kept my mouth shut. So I apologized, hugged him as hard as I could and said, "You are one awesome eighty-three year old."

He is.

January 2, 2014

MY SOLO CONVERSATION

I've learned not to interrupt Peter when he is thinking deep thoughts. But lately he doesn't even seem to like my talking to him when he is doing the daily crossword puzzle.

On Saturday, I was folding the laundry at the dining room table where he was working on the puzzle. I asked him a question that elicited a grunt that meant, "I don't want to be interrupted."

So, I returned to folding the laundry, and had the following conversation out loud, playing both parts myself:

Peter: "Thanks honey for doing all the laundry and changing the bed and cleaning the house. I know it's a lot of work."

Judy: "Oh, you're welcome. Would you like fish for supper tonight? My turn to cook."

Peter: "Sure, fish sounds good for supper. Thanks for offering to cook."

Judy: "By the way, I've decided to adopt a puppy from a shelter." (The last thing in the world that Peter would like is a dog.)

He looked up from his puzzle. "WHAT??!!!," he said.

At least I got his attention.

January 12, 2014

TASTING THE MARMALADE

Hi. I'm Judy's husband, Peter, and she has invited me to be a guest blogger again. Perhaps she thought that I might have some more wisdom to share about life in one's seventies, since I'm in my eighties and I've been through the full catastrophe. But I'd rather talk about life in my decade. Judy's next one.

This morning, at breakfast, I stopped reading the newspaper and paid attention to what I was eating – a good piece of bread, toasted, spread with unsalted butter and topped with orange marmalade. I've been ignoring my breakfast while reading the paper for years.

But when you're in your eighties, you realize that the number of breakfasts you're going to eat is finite. Oh sure, they've been finite all along, but small numbers are more finite than big ones. As there are fewer of them left, they are getting more precious.

It's not just the days that are getting fewer. So are the things I can do. I can no longer ride my bicycle to Harvard Square, let alone down the "D" roads of France. I can no longer see well enough to drive at night, and one of these days I won't be able to drive at all. I'm losing my sense of smell. My memory isn't what it used to be.

However, having less left is making what I still have more valuable. I think Martin Amis got it right when he said, "I find that in your sixties everything begins to look sort of slightly magical again. And it's imbued with a kind of leave-taking resonance."

I'm finding that leave-taking resonance in my eighties. I suspect that it's findable at any age.

March 2, 2014

THE OLDEST THING I NEVER GOT RID OF

On Thursday, I pulled my chocolate-brown wool slacks and brown and white tweed jacket from the depths of my closet. This was my go-to-work outfit on the coldest days for years, and it's been a losing candidate for the give-away bag every spring.

I wanted to look sharp for my Thursday session with the high school juniors I was helping with their applications for summer enrichment programs. And to be warm.

At breakfast, Peter didn't comment about what I was wearing. He almost never does, I think that is because he approves of my taste. I was trying to remember how long I had had that jacket. I interrupted Peter's paper reading to say, "I think the jacket I am wearing is the oldest thing I never got rid of."

We looked at each other. I waited for his response. But I was the one who said what we both were thinking, "except for…"

March 16, 2014

84!!!

Last Monday, the handsome thirty-five-year-old who swept me off my feet on July 13, 1965 turned eighty-four. To this day, my heart beats faster when I hear his key turning in the lock. His sandy-colored hair is now white and there is (a lot) less of it. He has a hearing aid (that he wears occasionally). His Parkinson's Disease has slowed his walk and made his fingers less nimble. But his quick wit, his sharp mind and his willingness to put up with me make me grateful for every minute with him.

But somehow this birthday, this age, feels different. This is his last year to be "young-old." At eighty-five, according to the medical literature, one becomes "old-old". Individuals age differently, but we are more aware than ever that we have to make each day count.

So I make plans to ensure that we always are looking forward to something wonderful. For example, we buy tickets for visits to our children months in advance. And we just re-subscribed to a music series that has its last concert in May, 2015. When you stop planning, you are giving up on your future.

With that in mind, I told Peter it was time to plan for a great birthday celebration twelve months from now. Knowing our kids, we need to get on their calendar way in advance. I asked him how he would like to celebrate his eighty-fifth. His reply, "By not celebrating." Often Peter's "no" response can be turned into a "yes."

I'm working on it.

June 9, 2014

SLOWING DOWN

If I had a nickel for everyone eighty or older who needs a regular day-time snooze, I'd retire. (But wait, I am retired!)

For quite a while, Peter would announce, "I'm sorry to say this, but…" or "I'm afraid I'm going to…" apologizing before heading upstairs for his almost-daily nap, usually around 2:00 p.m.

He doesn't apologize any more. And he shouldn't.

Other things have changed/are changing because of our age. I have been our designated night driver for years because Peter's glaucoma affects his night vision. And since his agility has diminished because of Parkinson's Disease, I usually drive when we anticipate having to park between two curbside cars. But lately, I seem to be driving more and more just because he prefers not to.

Some other changes in my 84-year-old husband—he eats less (not a bad thing) and more healthily (a good thing). And although he claimed that he was going to drink more gin as an old guy, he can't handle it, so wine is usually his alcoholic beverage of choice. And although he has always been a man of the mind, he seems a bit more introspective. Or maybe he just doesn't talk unless he has something meaningful to say (unlike the rest of us).

BUT, he is still the handsome, brilliant, funny guy who has loved and taken care of me for almost 50 years.

And that's what matters.

October 30, 2014

CAUGHT IN THE ACT

Peter and I met at work decades ago. I was more interested in him than he was in me, but I was determined to pursue him. I discovered that I had a good chance of bumping into him if I wandered by the candy bar machine in the hall near his office. He seemed to have quite a sweet tooth.

I hadn't thought about that aspect of my pursuit of Peter in a long time. Until recently. A couple of weeks ago I saw a yellow jellybean on the floor of our car. Odd, I thought, and I forgot about it.

Then last Thursday, Peter and I went our separate ways after our music class because he was going home and I was going to a lunch date. My friend Joanie and I lingered in the auditorium to talk to a couple of the musicians who had just played for us. Then we headed to a nearby CVS to do an errand.

As we approached the store, I saw Peter walking toward us. In his hand, he was clutching a bag of candied fruit slices. Caught in the act!

When I got home, I confronted him. "How often to you do buy candy?" I asked.

"Enough," he replied.

I smiled about it for the rest of the day.

November 2, 20/14

WE'VE HAD OUR TIME

When cyclists whoosh past us on our walks, Peter and I miss our twenty-five years of bicycling vacations. When we shiver in the late fall cold, we envy the young people outdoors in T-shirts. When we clumsily tap text messages while kids' thumbs fly, we feel ancient.

Then we remind ourselves that we've had our time.

The other day, we were discussing our health challenges (which thankfully are manageable) and whether or not we should make an appointment to meet our new primary care doctor so that she will know us as fit, active, non-complaining patients before we need her.

Even though we've had our time, we'd like her to help us have a little more.

December 21, 2014

SATURDAY SEX

I don't write much about sex. That's probably because I was born about five years before it was a subject we talked about in public.

I won't pretend to be an expert about the sex life of my peers. But for us, it's usually a Saturday morning thing. I think it's because our hands are too cold when we hop into bed on winter evenings. Plus, we're usually pretty tired. And even though we are retired, we have so much going on during the week that we have to get up pretty quickly on weekdays. So Saturday makes a lot of sense.

Last Saturday morning, we lingered especially long. Those moments together are very special and I said so to Peter.

"It's the highlight of my week," he responded.

March 26, 2015

THE ONLY CONSTANT IS CHANGE

My father died when my mother was sixty-nine years old. She lived seventeen years longer, missing him every minute. So when Peter turned eighty-five earlier this month, among the things I was grateful for was that at age seventy-seven, I still have him.

Throughout our marriage, I have seen my handsome husband as the man who could do anything. And did. But (no surprise) things change. We haven't been able to take the rigorous biking vacations we used to take since he was diagnosed with Parkinson's Disease eight years ago. Inveterate on-our-own travelers, we now go on guided tours. (At least we can still go!)

One of the hardest things for us both is that I am doing more of "his" tasks, like driving, doing chores that require fine finger dexterity, etc. And I find that I have to remind him of things more often than both of us prefer. Sometimes I fear that I sound like his mother. It's not what I would wish for.

Neither would he.

June 28, 2015

IN THE LONG RUN

Peter and I just completed our "end-of-life" documents. They spell out how we want to deal with the inevitable health issues that we will someday face. Not fun, but important.

We've indicated how much we want to know about our medical condition, the kind of care we would like, what aggressive treatments we would choose (or not), and who we would like to have with us in our last moments. These decisions are difficult and personal, but we know how important it is to make them and to write them down for our loved ones and doctors.

Although it is hard to define exactly what it means, we both believe that our quality of life is very important. For me, when I can no longer enjoy coffee ice cream, I've come to the end of my run…and it will have been a good one.

July 16, 2015

ANNIVERSARY

Fifty years and three days ago, a nice man gave a perfect stranger a ride to work. The perfect stranger needed transportation to her new job because her red Volkswagen Beetle hadn't arrived at the dealer on time and there was no available public transportation. Human resources (then called Personnel) at the firm arranged the pickup at the subway station in Harvard Square.

It must have been a "sign" when that nice man picked her up in his red Volkswagen Beetle. He and I have had fifty amazing years together (albeit only forty-seven of them as man and wife).

When I reminded Peter of our milestone, he gave me a big smile. I climbed onto his lap and shed tears of joy.

August 2, 2015

FORTY-SEVEN YEARS

After the 50th anniversary of our meeting a couple of weeks ago, our 47th wedding anniversary isn't earth-shaking news. But we celebrated it anyway.

We made a special dinner, preceded by a glass of red wine on our patio. There was a gentle breeze, and our backyard garden seemed especially beautiful lit by the setting sun. As we do more often at this stage of life, we noted how lucky we have been.

Peter raised his glass and made a toast to forty-seven more years. Since that's not going to happen, I suggested that we make the most of what's left and try to make a graceful exit when the time comes.

We drank to that.

November 8, 2015

PILLOW TALK

Scene: 10:30 p.m. A couple in bed, cuddling
Me: "You are so sweet."
Peter: "No, you are so sweet."
Me: "We're a very solid couple."
Peter: "I love holding you in bed. It's my favorite time of day."
Me: "That's because bed is the one place we can hold each other and be sure we won't fall over."
Curtain.

January 3, 2016

PETER'S ANNUAL UPDATE

As she has in past years, Judy has invited me to report on how things are going. The bottom line: They're going well, but not as well as they used to.

In my eighties, life is becoming a bit more difficult. Probably my biggest problem is my balance. I can't go down a flight of stairs without holding onto a banister. I've fallen a few times recently and, as a result, I'm much more cautious when I walk. One of these days, I'll probably start using a cane.

I have a hearing aid. I use reading glasses. I'm losing my sense of smell. I don't see well at night, and I can't drive after dark. I find it hard to park the car and, when I talked with my doctor recently, she suggested that it might be time to have Judy watch my driving to see if I should stop.

It all sounds rather grim, but it's not.

Although my mind is not what it used to be, it's still working reasonably well and that's a big plus. My remarkable young wife has taken over a lot of my tasks and that helps me (but not her).

But it's hard for me to ignore the fact that I'm going downhill. When you're young, you gain new capabilities as you age. You get old enough to drive, to have your own phone, and buy a beer. When you're in your eighties, you lose capabilities as you age. Fortunately, the losses aren't so noticeable as long as they're gradual. I feel like the proverbial frog that jumps out of the pot if it's full of hot water but sits there if the water starts off cold and is gradually brought to a boil.

Like frogs, we humans are designed to notice differences rather than absolute amounts. So, when you walk into a house in which somebody has been frying onions, you notice the smell because it's change from what you've been smelling outside. But after you've been in the house for a while, you no longer notice the smell because it hasn't changed.

So I may have woken up this morning a little stiffer than I was yesterday, but it was a small change. So I didn't notice it. What I did notice was the taste of my breakfast. That was a big change from the empty mouth I woke up with. So I noticed it and I enjoyed it.

Luckily my life still has lots of noticeable sudden improvements that I enjoy. And the worsenings have been gradual. But I'm not a frog. I need more than good breakfasts to keep me happy and luckily, I'm getting those things. Some of them I'm making for myself. Lots of them are provided by friends and family (particularly my wife).

I know that I'm lucky that the good times have lasted as long as they have and I know that they won't last forever. The changes for the worse may become more noticeable as they become more abrupt. And, one day, the water will come to a boil.

But today, I'm happy as a frog. Actually, happier.

March 6, 2016

24/7 WITH PETER

We're back home after our two-month escape from winter. We were ready to come back. We had great fun and it was wonderful to be away from the cold. But it was time to resume our normal life.

What I can't get over is how good every minute with Peter was. We've never been away for eight weeks before. With the exception of some long walks with female friends and the time Peter went to see *The Revenant* with a male friend, we were together 24/7. I have thought hard, but I can't come up with an angry word that we exchanged.

We have a comfortableness together that allows us to be in the same room, writing or reading, and sense when it is time to have a conversation or to go for a walk. I know not to interrupt him when he is writing, and he knows it's OK to interrupt me.

We are in tune, in sync, in love.

March 13, 2016

BIRTHDAY "BOY"

Thursday was Peter's birthday. He's well into being old-old. Even without his various conditions, reaching 86 would be something to celebrate. I think his positive and upbeat attitude enables his well-being. It doesn't hurt that, as I reported to him, just this week, two women told me how handsome he is—still!

I was very excited about my present to him. We had admired a small sculpture in a gallery in Florida. When we got home, I called and ordered it. The gallery agreed to ship it in plain wrapping, and although Peter saw the package at our front door before I did, he never asked what was in it.

When I gave it to him at breakfast Thursday, he didn't quite have the reaction I expected (namely, jumping up, throwing his arms around me, telling me how clever I was).

So he's not perfect. But, he's still a keeper.

June 9, 2016

Just an Ordinary Friday

We'd had a busy week. Our son Seth's visit involved lots of fun activities. On Tuesday after he left, we attended a conference and on Thursday evening, we went to a book party. So on Friday we took it easy, Peter and I each in our "office".

It was cloudy when we took a late afternoon walk in nearby Mt. Auburn Cemetery, followed by a glass of wine on our patio when the sun finally appeared. Everything was green. Our peonies were bursting from their buds.

Birds were devouring the berries on our trees. And our bunny friends ignored us as they chomped on our grass.

Later, watching the evening news, my eyes filled up twice—first over the joyous tears of a little girl whose birthday present was a doll with a prosthetic leg just like her own, and the second over the annual montage of graduation speeches, ending with the moment the U.S. Naval Academy's Class of 2016 threw their hats into the air.

Most of all, I was appreciating Peter. So grateful that we have this time together.

August 14, 2016

Daisy Purple Church

Lately, I have been going with Peter to his neurologist appointments. She is an excellent, thorough, and caring physician.

I go because:

1. Experts say it is good to take a family member with you to medical appointments, and I like to support Peter and listen with him.

2. If we bring his doctor a problem she has a solution, or at least some helpful suggestions, to deal with it.

3. I leave feeling happy that Peter is in her capable hands.

The appointments are long because she is very thorough. Early on, she always asks him where we are and what day and year it is. Then she gives him three words to remember. This time they were daisy, purple, and church.

When, near the end of his appointment, she asked him to repeat them, he remembered what they were.

Thankfully, so did I.

September 4, 2016

"Toto, We're Not in Kansas Anymore"

Judy Garland's famous line from *The Wizard of Oz* came to mind the other day. I was still fatigued from an over-busy August. I didn't like that it took me so long to bounce back.

Shortly thereafter, I heard two stories from friends that convinced me that I am not alone in feeling that I might have to slow down a bit.

One friend told me that she and her husband have had to cut short a lovely walk along the ocean that they had no trouble completing in past summers. Another, a seasoned traveler who had just returned from an anniversary celebration in Hawaii, complained of her first jet lag ever.

So if "Kansas" was our time of unbounded energy, like Dorothy, we're not there anymore.

However, our state is still pretty good.

9/15/16

Wrong Answer/Right Answer

Like an elephant, I never forget. And that means I still haven't forgiven Peter for not being able to identify the moment that he realized he was in love with me.

It was over last Thanksgiving that I gave our children a detailed description of the moment when I realized that I loved their father. I asked Peter to tell the kids when he knew he was in love with me. "I have no idea," he said. Wrong answer.

I thought of that exchange on Sunday when Peter was, as usual, deeply immersed in the crossword puzzle. I asked him which of the follow activities he preferred: *The New York Times* crossword puzzle or cuddling with me.

"Cuddling with you," he replied.

Got that one right.

October 9, 2016

To Move or Not to Move

Eight years ago when Peter learned that he had Parkinson's Disease, we thought we would have to move from our four-story home because of his potential mobility problems.

We began a fruitless condo search that lasted about five years. Two things have kept us where we are. One is that we never found the right condo and the other is that Peter is still handling the stairs fairly well.

But it's time to decide where to live when we can no longer be on our own. So when I saw a posting on a bulletin board looking for "seniors" who are struggling with this decision to be interviewed for a book on the subject, I signed up. I was hoping we might learn something to help us make our decision.

Of course, in a 45-minute phone conversation, we didn't get enough information to make a final decision. But here's what we learned. The people the researcher interviewed fell into one of two categories. Either they weren't "ready" to move or, if they were already living in a continuing care retirement community, they wondered why they had waited so long to make the move.

Interesting.

January 8, 2017

The Clanging of the Mailbox Door

Although it is a difficult subject, we have been talking about where we want to live when we are old-old, or in Peter's case, very-old-old. We love our home and if everything stayed the same, we'd never leave.

But everything won't stay the same.

So we are considering our options. Last month we visited a nearby continuing care place. It has an excellent reputation—from quality of the facility to the food to the administrators who have been there since it began, almost thirty years ago. We had lunch with friends who live there. They have a lovely apartment and are very happy.

But everyone is old—like us. A diverse community in age and other dimensions has always been important to me, and a continuing care community is not diverse. I felt very down when we left.

That particular place has a two-year wait list. So putting in an application would allow us to stay right where we are for another couple of years. And who knows what our situation will be then. We will also have time to consider other options.

When I closed the mailbox door after depositing the envelope with the application that will put us on their wait list, it made a loud clanging sound. It felt ominous.

March 9, 2017

AMAZING AT EIGHTY-SEVEN

Tomorrow is my husband Peter's eighty-seventh birthday. I don't recall thinking about what he would be like at eighty-seven when I met him many decades ago.

I know that I am lucky to still have him, and I think about that every day. He doesn't run marathons any more—in fact, he doesn't even walk all that well, and that's OK. He sometimes answers a different question than the one I ask because he doesn't hear as well as he used to, but usually I can laugh at that. Most important, we still agree on almost everything, and we laugh together a lot. We are accepting of the losses that come with aging and grateful for our amazing family and steadfast friends.

So Happy Birthday my sweetheart. And thank you.

3

ROOTS AND WINGS

Parents and Parenting

"Parenting is the easiest thing in the world to have an opinion about, but the hardest thing in the world to do."
Matt Walsh

In the almost fifty years that I've been a mother, I've learned that although the kids grow up, they remain our "babies." They're on their own, but the worrying doesn't stop. They're on their own, but the joy (and a bit of sadness) doesn't stop. Once a parent, always a parent.

Parenting is a tough job. From the moment of your child's birth, you are committed, and there's no quitting allowed. You have to show up. Every day. Your kids grow up. They have their own children and still, you are a parent.

We have been lucky with our kids. But we are careful not to take credit so that we don't have to take blame. I am sure we made some mistakes along the way, but I can't remember them. I know we did some things right like send them to a wonderful YMCA summer camp that helped turn them into the fine human beings that we think they are.

Worry is part of parenting. We checked on our newborns as they slept. We held our breath as they drove without us for the first time. We followed the ambulance to the emergency room after our goalie son collided with a soccer goal post. We've felt the pain of their romantic ups and downs. We feel their challenges even now.

Being a parent also made me appreciate my parents. My father had a tough childhood as an immigrant and he didn't have the educational opportunities he provided for his children. His life was his work and his family and he succeeded at both. My mother was the perfect housewife. A three-course dinner in our dining room on a freshly-ironed cloth tablecloth was the norm. Dinner always ended with a home-made dessert.

I wonder what my mother would have said about my still working at age seventy-five (not to mention our eating in the kitchen on placemats).

The old saying "We give them roots—and wings" captures parenthood well.

I never thought I would let our first-born cross the street alone. A travel writer now (among other things), often I don't know what country he's in. His brother, father of our two grandsons is the best dad I have ever seen, our daughter in law is a perfect partner in that regard. But that family, too, is a plane ride away, a plane ride we take as often as we can.

My mother once told me that she regretted allowing me to go away to college because I never lived nearby again. Having both our children live elsewhere is hard. But thanks to email and texting, to photos on smartphones, to Skype and Instagram, we manage.

So goes parenting, the hardest job I've ever had—and the best.

February 25 2008

Dad

I thought of my father when I woke up this morning.

Dad was a mystery in many ways. I have a photo of him before I was born, probably taken in the early 1930's. There he is, the epitome of debonair in his knickers, leaning against his Hupmobile, his Lucky Strike cigarette in his very long cigarette holder clenched between his teeth. Mother always said he was a ladies' man. I'm not exactly sure what she meant.

Dad left home to earn his living at age thirteen. His resume is very, shall we say, eclectic? There were tales of his starting the first indoor miniature golf course (a disaster) and many other undertakings before he settled down on a path that led him to be a successful state-wide manager of a life insurance company. As a salesman early in his insurance career, he was on the road a lot, but my mother could always open the front door at 5:00p.m. on Fridays, and he would be pulling into the driveway. If it was the right season, she would have the pot boiling on the stove for the fresh corn he would bring from a farm stand on his route home.

Dad never adjusted to retirement. He had only known work—no golf, no hobbies—and I think that may have contributed to his much-too-early-into- retirement death.

Even before his terminal cancer struck though, I remember him frequently remarking, "I ache all over."

This morning when I woke up, I ached all over and thought of my father, whom I still miss very much.

April 16, 2008

DAD, BASEBALL AND ME

I love listening to major league baseball. That's right—listening. On a radio.

Pretty strange, you might say. How can you not watch on TV? Well, for starters, we didn't have cable until yesterday, so except for championship games, I could only listen. And that was fine with me.

I think I prefer listening because that was one of my favorite activities with my father. When I lived in Cincinnati, I loved the Reds. When I was nine, we moved to Pittsburgh, and the first game I attended with Dad, I cheered for the Reds rather than the Pirates. But eventually, I became a huge Pirate fan. In those years, players stayed on teams much longer than they do today, so we got to think of people like Ralph Kiner, Danny Murtaugh, Vernon Law and Gus Bell as extended family.

Dad was the western Pennsylvania manager of a national life insurance company, and he had four season tickets for the Pirates just above the visitors' dugout, ostensibly to entertain his clients. But, as far as I can recall, he mostly entertained his family.

When the team was away, however, listening to the radio was what we did. I can picture us sitting in our tiny sunroom, bonding. The Pirates' announcer then was a man named Rosey Roswell, and he was a legend, perhaps best known for his response to a baseball leaving the park for a home run, "Open the window, Aunt Minnie, here she comes." We loved him, we loved the Pirates, and we loved watching together.

Of course, it only took a short time in Boston to switch my allegiance to my wonderful Red Sox. True, I have to learn a few new names every year, and I don't get to go to many games, but I consider myself a bona fide citizen of Red Sox Nation.

So last night I watched the game in our TV room. We have a new TV set with HDTV and cable that includes the Red Sox games. I watched about five innings. I wasn't crazy about all the dazzle, and missed the constant banter of the announcers. So I went upstairs and turned on the radio. The Sox won in the ninth. And I was very happy.

Dad would have been happy too.

June 1, 2008

On Beginning to be a Mother

I've been a mother for 38 years, as of last Thursday. That's not an unusual accomplishment. But I am astonished by how clearly I recall the details of the last few days of May,1970.

It was a very hot May, and it was hard to make my huge body do much. Back then, women didn't work until the first labor pain. I remember thinking that I had this baby inside me, and I would soon hold my child in my arms. But except for learning how to breathe through labor in Lamaze classes, I didn't know much about what would happen in between.

So in the afternoon of May 28, 1970 when I was standing in line at the S&H Green Stamp Redemption Center (remember those?), to pick up a new iron, the pressure in my belly didn't seem alarming. I pretty much ignored it. That evening we ate a big steak dinner (a bad idea that I did not repeat before the delivery of our next child), and we finally decided about 9:00 pm that these pains might be labor.

We arrived at the hospital at 10:00 pm for what turned out to be a very long and painful night. At 7:30 the next morning I held my now 38-year old son in my arms.

It could have been yesterday.

August 6, 2008

My Mother's Voice

While doing some serious moping around the house the other day, I heard my mother's voice in my head. "Nobody likes a sourpuss," it said, bringing back visions of me as a grumpy adolescent suffering because some boy hadn't called or I had suffered some other great setback in my teenage life. But I have this nagging doubt. Am I still a grump? I do have friends who seem to like me, but who knows? I thought of other times I hear her voice. For example, "Eat now because you might be hungry later." That sounds as odd now as it did then. Mother also had the habit, usually practiced as we were walking down the street, of saying "SB." That was her code for "shoulders back," her incessant reminder that I have bad posture. Despite her exhortations, I still have bad posture. And I still hear her saying "SB" in my head, alas. Or my all time favorite, "If you practice the piano, you'll always be popular because people like to gather around and sing." This statement would be made as I was listening to my friends playing kick-the-can outside while our kitchen timer sat on the piano ticking away until I was allowed to stop practicing and join them. By the way, in my entire adult life, I have never gathered around the piano to sing with friends, with the possible exception of Christmas parties. I asked my children for examples of what I say over and over that will remain in their heads forever. They couldn't come up with anything. I'll have to work on that.

November 23, 2008

THINKING ABOUT MY MOM

I've been thinking about my mother more than usual lately. On many occasions since she died nineteen years ago, I've wanted to ask her how she felt about life at my age. This usually happens when I experience a trauma of sorts and wish she were here to advise or take care of me.

Today I am wondering how she would react if she were back for a visit. Would she be surprised that we are going to inaugurate an African-American president? My guess is she would. But unlike her very conservative husband, I think she would be pleased.

I wonder if she could believe that at 70, I ride my bike to work every day. Two things there—riding my bike AND working at 70. She would have never expected me to exercise by choice, let alone lift weights three times a week.

Mom was a lady of leisure, although not rich. She volunteered for good causes, but the ladies played bridge and baked pies for their families during the week. They slept on ironed sheets and they didn't do junior years abroad.

When Mom was my age she had been a widow for two years. She missed my father very much and used to say that the hardest part of losing him was not having him with her to discuss the events of the day. I often wish that she could visit her grandchildren and great grandchildren. She would be so proud of them.

I'd also like to tell her that she was a terrific mother and I still miss her.

May 28, 2009

Four Generations in a Box

My grandmother Kate was born in 1869. I discovered that the other day while going through a box stored under our eaves and labeled "our good crystal". That box actually contains not crystal, but four generations of family pictures.

Kate gave birth to my mother in 1903 when she was 34, and my mother wasn't her youngest child. This, in an era when the average life expectancy at birth was 40 years. An interesting, but irrelevant fact is that I was born when my mother was 34, and our son Jeremy was born when I was 34.

My mother dutifully recorded the birth and death of her parents and all her siblings on an envelope stuck in with the pictures. Her father, Isadore, didn't die until 1960 so I actually got to know Grandpa pretty well. An interesting, but irrelevant fact is that he lived a lot of his life with one kidney.

There are pictures of my mother from high school and with her five siblings. There are several of my mother and father before they married.

Of course there is my baby book with all appearances of teeth recorded and endless pictures of my brother and me. There is the announcement of my birth and both of our children's birth announcements.

There are pictures of Peter and his family from Germany where he was born, including pictures of his grandparents who died in Auschwitz. There is an Hungarian passport picturing him and his younger sister Eva at about four and six (odd since they were not Hungarian). And there are lots of pictures of our own family that probably didn't make it into our many photo albums.

All those lives, packed in a box under the eaves.

There aren't any pictures of our grandchildren there because they are too young. But one day, there will be five generations in a box. Or maybe not—because most photographs reside on the Internet now.

Looking at them online won't be the same as holding those old photos in your hands and imagining what life was like in the olden days.

September 24, 2009

Weekend Dialogue

The cast: Jeremy, Grammy, Gramps, Leo (5) and Grady (2)

The scene: Son Jeremy and daughter-in-law Katrina's living room.

Props: Two plastic indoor kid-sized soccer goals.

Grady got both soccer goals first. Leo wants one. Grady does not want to share, and is having a meltdown. Jeremy calls Leo to come talk to him.

Leo: I know what you are going to say to me.

Jeremy: What I am going to say to you?

Leo: "Grady is only two years old. Even though he should share with you, is it worth having him scream and yell? Can't you just wait?"

Jeremy: You are right. That is exactly what I was going to say. You are going to be a good daddy some day.

Watching your children be parents. Does it get any better?

June 3, 2010

Thoughts on Being the Mother of a forty-four year old

Seth turned forty last Saturday. He lives five thousand miles away, but that didn't keep me from thinking about the "olden days" when he and his brother (who lives three hundred seventy-five miles away) were little. I decided to look for the journal I kept the week Seth was born. I am sure that I never threw it away, but I couldn't find it. However, I did find a yellowed day-by-day schedule left for our baby sitters when Peter and I went away for a week in January,1978. Here is an excerpt:

"Before school: Please put out Seth's clothes on his desk the night before. Give both kids clean everything except trousers which they can wear again if not too dirty. Seth will get up around 6:15 and read or come down and watch sports on TV. Jeremy will probably need to be wakened about 7:30 and he needs (or wants) help getting dressed.

After breakfast, Jeremy should have a vitamin and be reminded to go to the bathroom. Seth will need his hair brushed (brush is in drawer in hall). Also, they should brush teeth, if time. For snack, Jeremy should take four dried prunes and some raisins. Seth usually takes some juice in his thermos and two whole graham crackers."

That was thirty-two years ago. A far cry from living three hundred seventy-five and five thousand miles away.

August 30, 2009

Comfort Food

Years ago, when Peter and I often had dinner parties, we would always cook something new without trying it first. Although we took some chances, and no one went home hungry, these were not the kind of meals I grew up with.

Mother was a superb pie baker. Her flaky, buttery pie crust, was at its best in her apple pie. My father always claimed he needed to even off the edges of whatever was left in the pie plate, but we all knew he was just getting some extra for himself. Every dinner we had growing up was comfort food.

Lately, I find myself craving those meals. Nothing is more satisfying to me these days than a whole roasted chicken with thick buttery gravy made from its drippings. Or meatloaf and baked potato. Or good ole mac' and cheese.

If Mother could come to dinner now, she would feel right at home at our table as long as she wasn't expecting a tablecloth, three courses and a to-die-for apple pie.

August, 22 2010

WE ARE OUR PARENTS, OUR CHILDREN ARE US

I vividly remember an elevator ride in the tall, concrete apartment building that my parents retired to in Florida. I was alone in the elevator when a woman got on and said, "You must be Lillian's daughter—you look just like her." That was more than thirty-five years ago, but it is only recently that I have looked in the mirror, seen my mother looking back, and realized that the woman was right.

A couple of years ago, another elevator "moment" occurred. When I was in Washington DC on a business trip, I was commuting into the city with our son Jeremy. He suggested that I come say "hi" to his new boss at the Department of Education. Again, big building elevator ride. A colleague of Jeremy's got on the elevator. He looked at me and said, "You must be Jeremy's mother." It's true that Jeremy is the guy version of me—tall and slender, narrow face. But that obvious?

The latest look-alike is really a sound-alike. I work with a woman named Allison who could have been an opera diva. She had seen videos made by our son Seth on the *New York Times'* website. She sent me an email telling me that she enjoyed them and added, "He has your vocal cadence." Something only an opera singer would notice.

We are our parents, and our children are theirs.

February 10, 2011

THREE DAYS AND THREE GENERATIONS

Our grandson Leo's seventh birthday took us to Maryland. It was "Star Wars" all weekend--the theme of the birthday party, the gifts and finally the long-awaited permission to see the film. According to Leo, only one other boy in his first grade class hadn't seen "Star Wars". (It didn't escape Leo that his younger brother would be seeing it at age four, but Leo accepted that.)

Things are different now from how they were when our kids were seven. The accepted wisdom about party-size then was the age of the kid plus one equals the number of guests at a birthday party. There were fifteen children at Leo's.

And usually the parties were at home with possibly a magician. Leo's party was a production at a huge sports complex with games on the soccer field followed by pizza in "Party Room 1" followed by coins for the arcade games. The grandparents were exhausted.

Other memorable weekend events included my reading "Animal Magazine" crouched next to Grady on the bathroom floor while he pooped. I'm sure I never did that for our kids.

But perhaps the most memorable moment followed Leo's comment when his father asked him to throw away three used tissues Leo had left on the dining room table. Leo looked at his dad and in his most beguiling manner said, "Do I have to do EVERYTHING around here?!"

Leo's mother hates those words when Jeremy says them, and she does not want to hear them from her son. She was not pleased when I told her that "joke" was a staple in Leo's grandfather's repertory.

It's impossible to fight something that has been in the genes for three generations.

June 7, 2012

Like Mother, Like Son

Our son Seth is a writer who writes about travel. His mother is a graduate school dean who occasionally writes about travel. One could say I got there first, but Seth far surpasses me in talent, and, unlike me, he makes a living from it.

On Sunday, June 3d, his article "36 Hours in Oxford, England" appeared in *The New York Times*.

HOWEVER, nine years ago, his mother's article "Vacationing in a College Town—Oxford, England" appeared in *Arthur Frommer's Budget Travel Magazine*.

I was there first. Is that cool, or what?

August 5, 2012

SQUEAKY CLEAN

You know how it feels to have a great shower. Not when you are rushing to get somewhere, but when you have the time to be "in the moment" in the shower. You emerge feeling as clean as clean can be.

It was after one of those showers last week that I had a vivid picture of my dad sixty years ago, post squeaky-clean shower and shave.

We had only one bathroom in the house where I grew up. So we were keenly aware of when it was occupied or when it was not. Dad (who passed away forty years ago this month) would emerge from the bathroom, showered and shaved and emphatically announce, "I'm the cleanest person around. Who wants to kiss me?"

He'd have a towel wrapped around his middle, but more important, his head would be wrapped in a shaving towel à la Sheik of Araby. His signature after-shave lotion, Old Spice, permeated the hall as he emerged. My mother usually complied with the requested kiss.

Dad was impeccable about his appearance, probably because he had no money growing up. As a successful businessman, he wore only the finest high-end suits and ties. No hair was ever out of place, not a speck of dirt under a finger nail.

Squeaky clean.

November 16, 2014

"UNCLE MOM"

Our daughter-in-law Katrina loves Paris, so when she was offered an all-expenses-paid three-day trip there to join a friend celebrating her fortieth birthday, she had to go. She hesitated to leave the kids, but Jeremy urged her to go (especially since that got him off the hook for taking her there himself).

Jeremy was happy to be the full time parent when he wasn't working, but they needed someone to help get the kids to and from the bus stop on school days. Who better than his brother, Uncle Seth? Because he is on book leave from his job, Seth agreed to do the bus runs and be available for any daytime emergencies. The kids adore their uncle.

On the first day, Uncle Seth helped the kids make their lunches and drove them to the bus stop long after Jeremy had left for work. There were other kids at the stop, so Seth left. Big mistake. You are either supposed to stay with your children at the bus stop or ask another parent to watch them. Seth explained that when he noticed that there were more kids than cars, it seemed that others had dropped off kids and left. What he didn't think about is that many kids live within walking distance from the bus stop. First mistake. Would there be others?

That turned out to be the only blunder I heard about. The kids admitted they got some extra candy, but didn't mention any other extra privileges or problems while under Uncle Seth's care.

For me, my boys having quality brotherly time together warmed my heart. Jeremy reported that Uncle Seth was "awesome" at taking care of his nephews. For Seth, it was a taste of suburban life, so different than his New York City existence. From all reports, he had a great time too.

The boys sounded pretty excited when we talked to them on their way to the airport to pick up their mother. As for me, I was just relieved that all had gone well.

August 28, 2016

What Makes Me Cry

I seem to shed tears more often than the average person. I've been known to cry over TV commercials. So it was a given that, when Michelle Obama spoke at the Democratic convention about living as a black woman in a White House built by slaves, my eyes would fill up.

And our kids know that it doesn't take a lot to make me cry, so they write things on birthday cards and mother's day cards and notes that go into our Thanksgiving Day grateful jar that require me to have a tissue handy.

At our son Jeremy's wedding fourteen years ago, Seth as his brother's best man, made a wedding toast. He said his toast had three goals. I forget the first two, but the third was to make his mother cry. Not a problem.

March 12, 2017

Amigo Gringo

Our son Seth has produced and starred in about 150 videos for the Amigo Gringo channel on YouTube. Often viewed by half-a-million people, his videos are extremely popular in Brazil (they are in Portuguese with English sub-titles) and, while being helpful and informative, are also great fun. They are a guide to New York City, a guide to differences between Brazil and the U.S., and more. He writes them and stars in them with a professional cast. At the end of each episode, he gives a short lesson on the English language. People recognize him on the street in Brazil and sometimes in New York City where he lives.

So imagine our surprise and delight when he asked his parents to make a guest appearance on the channel. He posted a request on Facebook for questions he should ask his parents in an interview and received 152 suggested questions in just a couple of hours.

That's how we found ourselves sitting on a sofa in his apartment while he taped a video interview with us. Peter and I had to introduce the video in Portuguese. We did our best (poorly) reading a phonetic text from an iPad. Of course, the interview, in English, will have Portuguese sub-titles.

Seth did not tell us the questions in advance, but they ranged from how his father and I met to how we felt about Brazilian food to what's it's like having a son who plays a character who is a complete clod on YouTube. (The word that is used to describe him in Portuguese in the videos has been censored for the 70-something audience.)

Peter and I laughed our way through the interview. Not sure how we'll feel once it's edited, but it was so much fun to be part of our son's working of his magic.

4

IT TAKES A VILLAGE

FRIENDS

"Don't walk behind me. I may not lead. Don't walk in front of me. I may not follow. Just walk beside me and be my friend."
Albert Camus

Friends are the people who are there for you when you need them. They are the people you are there for too. Friendships matter even more as we age because social connections help us thrive. Whether it's my two friends from age four that I still see or new friends that I hope to get to know better, friends are pillars of my support system.

It's not easy being a good friend. It's time consuming. Sometimes it's darn inconvenient. But being a good friend is always the right thing to do.

March 4, 2008

Val

In 1989, my friend Valerie and her family moved away after thirteen years as our across-the-street-neighbor. I was on vacation when they left, so I didn't have to watch their departure. I do remember their arrival on our street, with their tiny infant twins fitting into one baby carriage, and the twins' older sister, about four, with a ton of bouncy blonde curls. Who knew then that nineteen years after they moved away, Valerie and I would still be talking on the phone every Sunday at 10:00 a.m.?

Val and I spent a lot of time together during those 13 years. We exercised in her basement twice a week to a Jane Fonda tape. Husbands and children swore we exercised only our mouths, but that wasn't true, although I did learn whom our son was taking to the prom during a Jane Fonda session long before he told me.

We always had Christmas dessert at Val's. One Christmas, we decided that since they had only girls and we had only boys, we should exchange a child for a week. (I think this stemmed from a conversation about which father was funnier.) I loved having another female in the house, and they welcomed our son as one of theirs.

Just last week, we learned that the bouncy-curls daughter may be joining the faculty of a college near one of our children. And might even live in his town. I don't know who was more excited, the children or the parents, as we envisioned another generation of neighbors.

Val and I plan to visit a spa together on the 20th anniversary of our Sunday morning phone calls. By then we would have talked on Sunday 1,040 times, give or take a few. Is that a record, or what?

April 27, 2008

Kathleen

On Monday my colleague and friend Kathleen told me she hadn't been feeling well over the weekend, some kind of stomach thing. On Tuesday, she still didn't feel great, but friends had told her of others who had been dealing with a similar lingering bug. On Wednesday, she saw a doctor who did some tests, and everything seemed fine. On Thursday, she felt lousy and stayed home. By Thursday night she was hospitalized with acute lymphoma.

Kathleen and I have been colleagues for 27 years. She has been a trusted and close friend from the beginning. Her contribution to our organization has been invaluable. She hasn't been as fortunate as I with her family life, but she loves her garden, she loves challenging projects; she reads biographies. She has a generous spirit and a good life.

So imagine how surprised I was when she told me that this cancer diagnosis was all right with her. She is a bit of a fatalist, and she accepts what comes her way. She is in a top-ranked hospital with excellent physicians, and she feels safe and cared for-- in a way, safer and more cared for than she does in her daily life. She says that she is now different than the rest of us and in a separate "zone".

Her future includes a hospital stay of uncertain-length, including aggressive chemotherapy. And who knows what after that? But nothing is expected of her right now, all pressure is off. Her friends and colleagues are hovering with offers of help and declarations of love.

We're worried. Kathleen is not.

May 15, 2008

KATHLEEN REDUX

Kathleen, was misdiagnosed. Her acute leukemia was not that at all. Coming to terms with the dire outcome of that disease, which she did so graciously, was unnecessary. Lymphoma, the correct diagnosis, is a disease that many live "with" for years. When you have a chance to live a full life instead of a few months or a year, it requires a different set of adjustments and expectations. I suspect that these adjustments will not be foremost on her mind until her cancer cells are blasted away.

But the cloud of Kathleen's illness had a silver lining. When colleagues, acquaintances and friends heard about her original prognosis, they rallied. Cards poured in. At work we started Team Kathleen to get her work done. Offers to cook, clean, bring meals to this very independent woman who lives on her own were organized. She felt loved by her friends and colleagues in a way she never has before.

Thankfully most of us are not faced with the kind of bad news Kathleen received last month. But how many of us get to find out how much we are loved the way she has?

That is her silver lining.

July 6, 2008

LEARNING FROM TINA, PART I

My friend Tina loves to give presents. She doesn't need an occasion. She just gives. And I have been the lucky recipient of many of her gifts. But more than that, I have learned from her how much fun it is to give, especially the unexpected gift. Once when I was with her at a pottery show, she admired a black vase. So I bought it for her. I don't know who was more pleased. When Tina sees something she thinks someone would like, she just buys it. The first person who said, "It's better to give than receive" definitely had Tina in mind.

Tina called today. She's planning to come see our grandkids when they are in town. She asked me for their exact ages. It wasn't until I hung up that I realized why she asked. I'm sure that she will be bringing something age-appropriate for them when she visits. I told Peter that I should call her back to try to talk her out of it.

"That wouldn't work with Tina," he replied.

July 16, 2008

WHAT CHRISTA SEES

Faithful readers of this blog know that my friend Christa is always upbeat, and that she is part of the couple with whom we have biked on vacation almost every year since 1989.

However, there is much more to Christa. For example, she sees things that we don't see. If we are biking along a country road in Italy, and there is an edible berry along the way, she will spot it. During the summer that we bicycled in the Alsace region of France, Christa spied a tree full of just-ripe cherries on our first day. Perhaps the cherries were not meant to be publicly available, but that would never stop her. Thanks to Christa, we ate lunch under a just-found cherry tree every day.

Christa and Gordon came to visit us in our rental house in the Berkshires last week. While walking across the deck to the front door with her suitcase, Christa stopped and pointed out the berry bushes along the brook below. That evening our dessert included the freshest black raspberries you can imagine. We hadn't even seen them.

I asked Christa why she notices things others don't. Her answer was interesting. When she was a tiny child in Germany during World War II, her family didn't have enough to eat, so they encouraged the children to find berries or food of any kind. Also, in Germany, children study nature more. School children keep a book of grasses one year, wildflowers the next. And finally, Christa is a professional photographer, taught to see what others do not.

She is very good at it.

September 28, 2008

Make New Friends, But Keep the Old

"…One is silver and the other gold." So go the words of an old song we sang last night with Gordon and Christa and Ted and Emilie, who have been our friends for over forty years. Lingering over dinner at Gordon and Christa's New Hampshire lakefront home on a stormy September night, we talked of politics, the financial crisis, our children, ourselves.

Away from the obligations of our daily lives and full of good food and wine, we suddenly started singing songs of our youth—"Your Hit Parade" songs, show tunes, camp songs. The others' voices were strong enough that I could sing out off key and no one minded.

We sang "Mona Lisa, Mona Lisa, men have loved you…" We sang "How Much is that Doggie in the Window?" and "Good Night Irene." We sang "Why Don't You Believe Me?" and our favorites from "Oklahoma" and "My Fair Lady." We sang "White Coral Bells" and other camp songs.

We should celebrate the past and sing with our friends more often. New friends are wonderful, but old friends are gold.

June 27, 2010

WHAT WOULD MURIEL DO?

I've been thinking about my friend Muriel. For thirty years, we were the best of friends, even though she is fourteen years older than I am. We always seemed to be able to solve each other's problems.

Over the past few years, she hasn't done so well. She has lost her husband of more than fifty years. I just heard through a mutual friend that she is having short-term memory problems, and needs an aide to help her read her mail.

I have a copy of an essay that Muriel wrote about how she felt about being in her seventies. She started the decade with a white-water rafting trip in the Grand Canyon. But she was feeling less adventurous as the years went by. She wrote about how much she enjoyed exercising and the memoir-writing classes she taught. She wrote about losing friends and the looming "statistical scoreboard." But she was happy.

Now, I am in my seventies, feeling less immortal, and wondering what I'll be like in fourteen years. But I am still asking myself, "What Would Muriel Do?

February 12, 2012

CLOSURE

I got a call from Muriel's daughter last Monday. She and her husband had moved across the country, but were back because her mother died on Saturday. Although I had been missing Muriel and "mourning" her for a few years, it was hard to hear that she was really gone. She had been such a force in my life, the big sister I never had.

I talked with Wendy for a long time. I caught up on all the siblings and grandkids. Wendy gave me her new email address, and we promised to stay in touch.

We hung up, and then I cried.

October 15, 2014

RECONNECTING

More than thirty years ago, I worked closely with a wonderful col-league at the Harvard Kennedy School. Ours was among the best work relationships I have ever had. She went on to a successful career elsewhere, and we lost touch. A couple of weeks ago, I learned something about our former boss that I *had* to tell her.

I tried to find her on the Internet. She wasn't on *Facebook*. She wasn't on *Linkedin*. This was going to be harder than I expected. It didn't help that her last name is Jones. Finally, through a Google image search for her and her husband, I found a picture of them at a fundraiser and learned where she works. I sent an email to the firm, explaining that I was a for-mer colleague trying to reach her and asked that they forward my email to her. Success at last!

We talked on Thursday. We chatted and laughed just as if it were thirty years ago. Forty minutes later, I had to end the conversation to get to my music class. We were definitely not finished. We promised to stay in touch.

After music class, I had lunch with another person from my past, the editor of the many travel articles and personal essays I had written for *The Boston Globe* in the 90's. When I saw her mentioned in a newspaper article about adjusting to retirement, I managed to get in touch with her too. We had a great time chatting about life's changes.

My music class that day had been a wonderful live performance of part of Handel's *Messiah*.

Some days are almost too good to be true.

November 6, 2014

DINNER WITH FRIENDS

More than forty years ago Peter interviewed for a teaching position with the chairman of Boston College's Computer Science Depart-ment, Jack Neuhauser. That interview led to more than thirty wonderful years of teaching at BC. And some lasting friendships.

We hadn't seen his former boss (now President of St. Michael's College in Burlington, Vermont) in years, and since we were having other BC friends for dinner, we asked him to join us.

Catching up on kids and grandkids and life in general was great. But the most memorable moment for me was when Jack recalled his phone conversation with Peter setting up that job interview so many years ago. Jack asked Peter, "Do you want me to tell you how to get to my office?" Peter replied, "If I can't find it on my own, you shouldn't hire me."

Thus began a great friendship, a great career, and some wonderful memories.

January 18, 2015

MY FRIEND INVENTORY

Friendships have been on my mind lately. It didn't take all the research that's out there about the importance of friends as we age to convince me that they are crucial to our well-being.

Here's my inventory of friends:

Friends I've known the longest—both named Barbara—both known since I was four years old.

Friends from high school: Two live in Greater Boston, and we talk regularly.

College: My closest college friend now lives less than two miles away. I love having her nearby. We've shared so much over the years and still are sharing.

Work: Close work friendships are harder to keep up now that I am retired, but I see three friends regularly and have lunch occasionally with others.

Former neighbors: My across-the-street neighbor in the house where our children grew up moved away in 1989. Twenty-five years later, we still talk almost every Sunday. And in the last few months, Peter and I have got together with two other friends from that neighborhood even though we've been gone for twenty years.

New friends: I think I started to think more about friendships because of our newest friends. We met them in an elevator just a year ago. They are Canadian. They are gracious and loving and generous. We saw them in Toronto last summer. Earlier this week, they gave a party for us here in Florida so that we could meet all their friends. It's wonderful to have new friends that are so special.

I am grateful for all my friends, especially my best friend of all. His name is Peter.

January 24, 2016

OLD FRIEND, NEW FRIEND

I lost touch with my friend Joanna when she moved to western Massachusetts several years ago. This year, by chance, she and her husband are renting a condo in the same building that we are on Longboat Key in Florida.

Once we found each other, Joanna and I caught up during a long walk along the beach. We reminisced about Brown Junior High School's wacky 1983 production of "Anything Goes", costarring her daughter Jennifer and our son Seth. We laughed about our Sunday school carpool. The only people who hated getting up early for it more than we did were our children. We talked at length about our current lives and some of the challenges we face. There is nothing like old friends chatting to make a long walk short.

Later that day, Peter and I had a glass of wine with a new friend that we had met at our condo complex's Trivia night. She lives in the same town as our son Jeremy and his family. We barely scratched the surface of our histories, but we know that this is a new friendship that we will value.

Having an active social life is good for us as we age. Old friends, new friends. All friends.

March 3, 2016

LEAVING THE 70'S

Friends who met as undergraduates and have been married forever gave a party for their joint 80th birthdays last Saturday. We've known them for some time, but have become closer in recent years, and we were delighted to be invited to celebrate with them.

Many things made this event special. For one, the hotel got the date wrong. It had the party on its schedule for one week later. Imagine arriving at 5:30 p.m. to host a 6:00 p.m. event you have planned for months, friends and family having flown in from near and far, to find ... nothing. (Actually, the photographer who wasn't provided by the hotel got the date right and was there.)

But the hotel pulled it off. People came back from their nights off and by 6:30, it looked like a party. And it was perfect—cocktails and hors-d'oeuvres, dinner, flowers, and even a gorgeous cake, prepared from scratch, and ready in time for dessert.

We loved meeting our hosts' charming children and grandchildren whom we had heard so much about. We discovered that their daughter-in-law had worked with our son Jeremy at a consulting firm twenty years ago and that her kids are now at the same summer camp that our kids attended as children.

Perhaps best of all, in this time when we tend to hear more bad news than good, it was an evening filled with love and joy.

July 24, 2016

The Wisdom of the Aged

When we spend time in New Hampshire at the lake-front home of our friends Gordon and Christa, we have very deep and meaningful conversations ranging from politics to history to whether to cut off both ends of fresh string beans before cooking them.

Last weekend, we were joined by their friend Jean and our profound discussion yielded some tenets of parenting that I feel compelled to share. They need no explanation.

1. A mother's place is in the wrong.
2. If you want to get along with your grown children, live far away and send money.
3. If you have to live nearby, keep your mouth shut and your purse open.

We also talked about politics, concluding that this was like no other election year and promises to become more unusual as it progresses. We limited the talk about our aches and pains to advising Christa on how to treat the insect sting on her eyelid. We ate too much.

Another great weekend.

July 28, 2016

Coda to the Wisdom of the Aged

Left out of the last 70-something post about profound subjects discussed in our recent New Hampshire weekend was our important conversation about foods we hated as children. We agreed that cooking has become much more imaginative in our generation, probably thanks to Julia Child initially and now to the many cooking channels on TV and the zillions of recipes available on the Internet through Epicurious and other websites.

But still, what we hated tells us something about our upbringing. As children…

1. Jean hated liver and onions. In her family, you finished what was on your plate. Period.
2. Peter hated stewed lungs (whatever those are).
3. Gordon could not tolerate fried eggplant.
4. For me, it was the (not-fresh) fish that made its way to Pittsburgh from some far-away ocean and was only edible when smothered in ketchup.

But it was Christa who was born in Germany at the start of the WWII who startled us with her reply.

"We ate whatever we could get."

I wondered what our kids having this discussion in 2050 would be saying about what they hated to eat as children…

September 1, 2016

HARVEY!

Eight months ago our wonderful friend Harvey was diagnosed with a rare form of cancer. His doctors told him not to look it up on the Internet because people with this disease don't survive. For the next few months, his life was a living hell of hospital treatments, infections, and middle-of-the-night visits to the emergency room. He could eat no food not cooked in his home. He could have no visitors for fear of more infections. It was grim.

On Sunday, Harvey and his wife Tina came by for a short visit, and stayed for more than two hours. No, he isn't cured. And yes, there have been setbacks along the way. But he has survived the harshest of treatments and his cancer is in remission. His blood cells have been harvested so that when he is strong enough he can have a stem cell transplant, his only chance for a real cure. He walks, he exercises strenuously and he has gained back the weight (and the hair) he lost. He is the Harvey we know and love.

Eight months ago, he thought he would never step into the ocean again. Last week, he and Tina went to the beach and did just that. In January, he thought he'd never see their vacation home again, and he will be there for the Labor Day weekend.

The stem cell transplant hasn't been scheduled yet—his doctors need him to be in even better shape than he is. There is always the fear that his cancer will return and he won't be able to have the transplant at all. And, of course, if he has it, it may fail.

But that doesn't stop Harvey. He has made a reservation to spend two weeks at their favorite winter get-a-way next February.

Harvey and Tina and Peter and I have spent New Year's Eve together for as long as I can remember. We take turns cooking elegant dinners for each other. This year it's my turn.

I'm planning the menu.

October 16, 2016

The Aprons of Yesteryear

While waiting for my learning-in-retirement class to begin the other day, the subject of aprons came up. The discussants of this highly intellectual topic were my high-school friend Ruth, who by coincidence is a member of my learning-in-retirement program, and me.

Our class is studying 1908 and 1928, two important years in American culture. Baseball, Henry Ford, and Orville and Wilbur Wright have been among the subjects we've discussed.

I'm not sure how Ruth and I got on the topic of aprons, but we were reminiscing about our high school Home Economics class (long after 1928) and wondering whether such a class exists in high schools today.

Both of us distinctly remembered the aprons we sewed in class. They had a wide pocket below the waist and some rickrack stitched across the top part across our chests. Mine was a happy fabric, 100% cotton, a cream-colored background with a tiny-multi-colored-flowers pattern. I can picture it as if it was yesterday.

We also "learned" to cook. I think the first thing we made was oatmeal, but maybe it was tuna fish casserole. I am sure it was something beige-colored. I know that the best thing we made was peanut brittle.

We're not sure what the boys in our class did in their Home Economics class (which was called "Shop") but we think they made bookends.

Not sure how well making an apron prepared me for life, but I know I haven't thought about it for sixty-five years.

December 26, 2016

My New Relationship

I'm still adjusting to the end of my more-than-thirty- year-relationship with Kelly who started cutting my hair when she was eighteen. Having a new hairdresser who is less than forty-five minutes away is a good thing, but the downside is not having Kelly in my life.

My new hairdresser, Linda, and I still don't have my hair quite right. But after three visits, we're getting there. It takes time to develop a friendship too, especially with such a different person. Lebanese, lots of cussing, strong opinions, enormous breasts, each with its own name, so nice to the mailman who visited each time I've been in her shop. My neighbors who have been going to her for years love Linda, so I am hopeful that eventually I will too.

I sent Kelly a Christmas check last week, and from her thank-you email, I realized how well she knows me. Eight years ago, she was the first non-family member I told about Peter's Parkinson's Disease. Here is part of her email last week:

> "I know the love you have for Peter is immeasurable. It's hard to imagine how much your life is affected and changing due to his Parkinson's. I also know this has to tear you up, break your heart, frustrate and anger you, and for that I am sorry, and saddened."

Kelly can see things about me that even I don't see. She is a hard act to follow. She will always be my hairdresser in my heart.

5

WHAT'S NEXT?

RETIREMENT

"Often when you think you are at the end of something,
you are at the beginning of something else."
Mr. Rogers

For years, friends asked me if I was ever going to retire. "We could travel in the off-season," said our travel buddies. "If you retired, you could spend more time with your grandchildren," said their father. "Keep working," said Peter who had retired from his tenured faculty position at Boston College at age 75. "You love your job too much—work as long as you can."

And I did.

My decision to retire was one of the hardest I have ever made. I was 70 before I started thinking about it. I spent five years thinking.

Soon after my 75th birthday, I acknowledged that the place I had loved for 33 years wasn't as much fun as it used to be. I didn't want to write another performance evaluation or plan another budget. Yet I couldn't imagine not being surrounded by smart graduate students from more than 80 countries and the brilliant faculty members who taught them.

I had a great idea, or so I thought. I found a way to leave without leaving. In May of 2013, I asked to join the incoming mid-career master's in public administration class as the oldest student ever. The Dean agreed, admitted me, said I could attend part-time, and awarded me a full scholarship.

Six weeks into the school year, I was miserable. My poorly-thought-out-decision to become a graduate student left me feeling completely disconnected. I found myself sneaking into school, and hiding out in the library between classes, trying to avoid my former colleagues. I was no longer essential to the operation of the school and I was reminded of it every minute.

And so I withdrew.

Retirement had removed my infrastructure and my foundation. The platform I stood on disappeared, and I had not given enough thought to what would replace it. The early days of my retirement were very difficult for me. I would do it differently, given another chance. I had trouble accepting that I, who counsels others as a professional, had not made a solid plan for my own future.

March 24, 2008

REHEARSING RETIREMENT

Yesterday, I tried out retirement. I had just turned 70. I didn't plan the day with retirement in mind. I just needed to get my non-working life in order. Things pile up (literally), and I needed some time at home.

I accomplished the following: I finished an article with an approaching deadline and wrote a query letter proposing another. I cleaned out some over-stuffed files and desk drawers, making difficult decisions, such as whether or not to throw out every Mother's Day card I ever received. (I didn't.) I ate a leisurely lunch at a real table, rather than inhaling lunch at my desk. I argued with Peter over disposing of our collection of a dozen cans of paint that don't match anything, but sit in a corner of our basement in a shroud of dust. (I lost.) And mirabile dictu, I didn't check my work email once.

It rained all day, and I never left the house. Is this what retirement would be like? I don't think I'm ready to find out.

October 9, 2008

OLD FOLKS TALK

At work, I am surrounded by people who are younger than I am. Since the mission of our school is to make the world better, there's a lot of talk about problem-solving in the present and challenges for the future. But no talk of aging.

So last weekend, away with two couples we have known for decades, I was struck by how different our conversation was. We reminisced about the good old days. We talked about our kids and their kids and what their futures hold. We spent a couple of hours that rainy afternoon sharing our thoughts about aging. We decided that although walking into a room and forgetting what we were looking for is a sign of incipient dementia to us, young friends do the same thing without giving it a second thought. And we talked of our fears of a bad death, and what we would do if faced with that situation.

We talked about what good luck we have had in our lives compared to the world at large, or even compared to some friends who have had multiple disappointments and losses.

It all may sound depressing. But it wasn't. We know we've had a great run, and we will make the most of whatever future time we are lucky enough to have.

Still, I was happy to go to work on Monday and talk about how we can make the world better.

March 28, 2010

WORK VS. RETIREMENT

The other night a colleague gave me a ride home from work because I didn't have my bike. The next day she asked if I minded answering a personal question. She said that when she had dropped me off at home, Peter was in front of the house. She noticed how warmly we greeted each other (after all these years). She was curious to know why, now that he is eighty, I don't leave my job to spend more time with him since we don't know how much time we will have together.

When I mentioned our conversation to Peter that night, he replied "For better or for worse, but not for lunch."

But my colleague's comment stayed with me, so I pressed Peter on this subject. I asked him if he wanted me to be with him more. I told him that if he wanted to take a trip around the world, I would quit my job. But he doesn't want to do that. Peter is a man who has a wonderful life of the mind. Teaching and learning is what makes him happy, whereas I am happiest problem-solving with people. So I belong at work, and he belongs with his life of the mind.

December 11, 2011

WHAT, ME RETIRE?

Friends, family, and even strangers ask me when I plan to retire. (My colleagues never ask which is a good thing.)

I'm old enough, but a couple of years ago I said "no" to a generous retirement package because I love my job. However, the day will come when I will leave it, hopefully standing on my own two feet.

There are times when I think I should just set a date. But I'm not ready. At seventy-three, I can say with conviction that I won't be working ten years from now. Should I retire in June? A year from June? When I am seventy-five?

On Wednesday, I attended the annual holiday dinner hosted by our Executive Dean. Every year we do a Yankee Swap at dinner.

This year I got the gift no one wanted, recycled by the person who didn't want it last year. So now, I can say with certainty that I will still be in my job a year from now. I can't imagine missing next year's holiday dinner when I will be able to re-gift that Christmas tree hat with its flashing colored lights.

July 18, 2013

AM I THE LUCKIEST PERSON?

I've never sought the spotlight. I don't like to be the center of attention. I just try to show up--on time, dressed and ready to play, as a beloved colleague used to say.

So on Monday when the announcement of my transformation from Associate Dean of Students to student went out to the faculty and staff of the Kennedy School, I wasn't prepared for the flood of amazing email responses. It felt like being at my own funeral without being dead.

People thanked me, called me a pillar of the School and wondered how the School could run "without me." (I'm sure it will do just fine.) They thought that becoming a student was a brilliant idea and a wonderful way to exit gracefully. They used the words "bold" and "fearless." The responses were astonishing. I was a basket-case of mixed emotions.

I think I will be the oldest graduate of our master's program, but I am sure I am the luckiest person ever admitted.

August 15, 2013

TEN MORE DAYS

Thirty-three years at my job. That is approximately 8,250 working days. And I have only ten left.

I look around my office, my home-away-from-home. On my walls I have two watercolors, two large prints and a bunch of awards. On the credenza next to my desk, I have an engraved glass plaque, given to me in 1999 by our Mexican alumni association. It thanks me for my "unvaluable" contribution to our Mexican students. (I don't know how to say "invaluable" in Spanish so I am not complaining about their English.) It's next to a certificate from Harvard, thanking me for twenty-five years of service. On top of my bookshelves are family pictures that I change annually, the old ones saved in a folder in my desk.

Yesterday, I took photos of my office walls with my cell phone so I don't forget what they looked like. Over the past two weeks, I've spent the time between meetings sorting through my files. I'm not nearly done, but I will be by August 30th.

It's a bit scary.

September 29, 2013

LAST MONDAY

While we were out of town visiting the kids last weekend, no magic elves did our laundry, watered our plants or went grocery shopping for us. So it was nice not to have to rush off to work on Monday.

Somehow, I managed to fritter away the morning on those undone weekend chores. In the afternoon I had a medical appointment and did some reading for my management class.

It wasn't until 8:00 p.m. that I realized I had spoken to a total of three people all day – Peter, the gardener who was trimming our neighbor's bushes and the woman who did my mammogram.

On a normal Monday before I retired, I would have had numerous encounters with colleagues and solved a bunch of problems for students.

It's quite a change.

October 13, 2013

SIX-WEEK REPORT

It's been six weeks since I retired. With a bit of help from William Bridges' book, *Transitions*, I now understand why it has been hard for me.

According to Bridges, transitions are difficult, no matter how sure you are that you are making the right move. Leaving a job you like is an adjustment. Going back to school is also an adjustment. And what did I do? Both at once. I have no doubt that it was time for me to leave my job. I have no doubt that I am lucky to be able to use my retirement to stretch my mind.

But now I get it that it is not as easy as I thought it would be.

October 27, 2013

RECALCULATING

If you have a GPS in your car, you know that when you don't follow directions, and you hear a menacing "Recalculating!" it's not good news.

I have spent the last couple of weeks "recalculating" my life, and that hasn't been good news either. I have reluctantly accepted that my decision to be a 75-year old graduate student was a poor one. I wrote earlier that I wanted to "taste the candy" by taking classes at the "candy store" where I had worked so long, and that seemed like reason enough to enroll.

But the enormity of the change (from a more-than-full-time job where I was important – to a graduate student where I wasn't) in just 48 hours didn't enter into my calculation. I listened to my heart and ignored my head.

I was doing very well in my classes. But I didn't feel like a student. I felt like an administrator pretending to be a student. And that didn't feel good. So last week, I withdrew.

My recalculation is a work in progress. I am giving myself some breathing time. I know that there is a right path for me toward a rich retirement in which I can give to others in gratitude for all the good things

I have received.

I will take my time, but I will find it.

October 31, 2013

Lasting Memories

At the summer camp I attended, they always served roast beef for dinner on the last night. I suspect they thought that when our parents asked us how the food was at camp, we would think about our final banquet and forget about the creamed-chipped-beef-on-toast dinners that we hated.

And so it was with my job. Now that I have been retired for two months, only the good things about it come to my mind: how much I loved working with the students, how smart and committed my colleagues were, and the importance of the mission that inspired us all.

However, when I dig a bit deeper, there are some things that I don't miss. I don't miss writing performance evaluations or justifying my budget. There were some non-fun committees I served on, and there was the time when we had to cut back our staffs. There are even one or two people I don't miss.

Like camp, although it served an occasional chipped beef dinner, it was a prime ribs experience.

November 3, 2013

Routine Problem

The 50-hour workweek of the job I just retired from required me to be super-organized. Saturdays were devoted to laundry, plant watering, grocery shopping and other errands. Sundays were my real break from the frenzy of the rest of the week. I loved Sundays.

I haven't developed my retirement routine yet. So I don't even know what day of the week it is. For example, I watch the evening news on TV. When I commented to Peter last weekend that I thought it was unusual for the weekday news anchor to be on the air on a Saturday rather than his regular weekend replacement, Peter informed me that it was Friday.

And then there are our plants, always watered before breakfast on Saturdays. For the last two weeks, it took me until late afternoon to realize that it was Saturday, and I had forgotten them.

I have decided that I need to pay more attention to what day of the week it is and I have found an easy solution. It's my bright red pill container. It is divided into seven sections, each marked with a letter.

M,T,W,T,F,S,S

November 17, 2013

WARDROBE

I used to change into my comfy clothes within moments of coming home from work. I might have stopped on the way upstairs to plant a kiss on Peter's cheek, but nothing else could stand in the way of my journey to comfort.

My standard at-home apparel was a pair of jean-like Bermuda shorts and a T-shirt in the summer and LLBean's elastic-waisted black-cotton-and-lycra slacks and a turtleneck the rest of the year. My feet preferred my Birkenstocks at home no matter what the season.

On weekend days I would upgrade to a good pair of jeans and a top that was appropriate for wherever our errands might take us. I loved the switch to my non-work-day wardrobe just because it was so easy. No standing in front of the closet trying to choose which outfit I hadn't worn for a while.

Things are different now that I am retired. I can (and do) wear jeans almost every day. My work outfits (with the exception of my navy blazer and maybe one or two other things) remain in their cleaning bags in the guest room closet. I plan to take most of them to Dress for Success, an organization that helps disadvantaged women enter or re-enter the job market.

But not quite yet…

February 9, 2014

A New Life: Chapter One

I've never reinvented myself in any organized way. My life just happened. I've had a happy childhood, a good education, a super-good marriage, outstanding children and a great career.

Retirement is a whole new thing. Letting go of the past and figuring out what to do next has been a challenge. But I think I've got it now.

I have begun working with an inner-city charter school that has had great success in getting its graduates into college. I am going to help the juniors and seniors go through the application process.

Next week, I begin courses in a life-long learning program. I will take "Understanding Poetry" because I know nothing about poetry except that I don't like it. I hope to change that. And I will take a course on China's transformation in the twenty-first century, something else I know nothing about.

In April, I will begin training to be a volunteer consultant to non-profits, particularly in executive coaching.

Is it too much? Not enough? Just right? I'll find out.

March 20, 2014

So Much To Learn

I'm finding that the time I spend volunteering with my inner-city charter school kids is an education for me. I'm there to help them, but they are helping me.

I am learning about what it's like to be taunted by the kids in your neighborhood because you like school. I'm learning about how distracting it is when your parents fight all the time. I'm hearing about their long commutes and the effort they put in to attend a school that they believe will offer them more opportunities.

I'm hearing that they're worried about leaving home this summer to attend a three-week enrichment program at a college a few hundred miles away. "But, I've never been away from my mother," said one. And how one family can't come up with the $100 deposit *even though they will get it refunded.*

The students tell me they will not apply to schools in Florida because they've heard Florida is racist. One described feeling uncomfortable at Disneyworld, not because of staff, but because of the other visitors' behavior toward them.

I am learning about struggles that neither I nor my children had to face. And I am loving these kids who find the energy and determination to succeed when the odds are not in their favor.

April 3, 2014

RETIREMENT UPDATE MONTH SEVEN

I'm making progress on getting used to retirement. People told me that I would be busier than ever once I got the hang of it. They also said it would take at least a year for me to adjust, maybe even longer because I loved what I did. But they assured me that I would eventually welcome having more control over my time.

What I Like So Far:

- Not having to set the alarm every morning. And when I do set it, it's not for 6:05 a.m. (Also going out on weeknights is easier.)

- Non-weekend grocery shopping. I see lots of retirees, mothers with strollers AND no long checkout lines.

- Doing only what I want to do (or at least stopping what I don't want to do as soon as I know it).

- Learning stuff I didn't know I wanted to learn, even some things about myself.

What I Don't Like So Much:

- Retirement doesn't make life stress-free.

- I haven't been able to shed my "Type A" personality. A day sitting around with a good book doesn't work for me.

- Not seeing the fruits of my labor as I did at work. (Peter might disagree since part of my labor is making him happy.)

Retirement is a journey.
Isn't everything?

April 20, 2014

BEING OLD

In spite of what the world sees (and the mirror tells us), deep inside most of us seventy-somethings feel like we're still forty.

We aren't.

Until I retired last fall, I wasn't "old". Was it working with students that kept me feeling young? Or was it the sense of identity and purpose that came with my job?

When I started at my learning-in-retirement program, I wondered what I was doing with all those old folks. How could I be one of them? It turns out that those "old folks" have rich experience, tremendous energy and generosity of spirit, regardless of their wrinkled faces and faltering steps. We learn from each other every day.

I am a lucky "old" person. I take only one pill. I still ride my bike and I still have my love of so many years.

But...I am old.

September 14, 2014

BACK TO SCHOOL

One of the joys of living in a college town (besides having had a rewarding career at one of its colleges) is attending free events that range from sheer entertainment to intellectual challenges.

And, as I am finding out this fall, you can also go to class. Not to doctoral seminars, or over-subscribed classes, but a polite request to a faculty member will usually get you a slot to audit a course if there is space.

That's why Peter and I are spending two mornings a week with a bunch of undergraduates learning to appreciate five great classical musical pieces with the help of a gifted instructor.

We got to class early the first day, introduced ourselves to the professor and asked if we could sit in. He graciously agreed and then told us that he loved auditors because they showed up on time (and haven't just fallen out of bed, and raced to class with hair still wet from the shower).

And there's another bonus. Observing undergraduates is fun. The first day there was a lot of, "Hey, how was your summer?" "Do you like your dorm set up?" "What are you taking?" Very different than our conversations with our peers. And they have different distractions than we had in college. There were a lot of open laptops. Taking notes, or surfing the Web, I wondered? The undergrad next to me thumbed his phone for a while, but after that he seemed engaged.

At Thursday's class, things got serious. Harder material. Open laptops forbidden. And a chance to experience music more deeply.

The class lasts 53 minutes. I never look at my watch.

October 1, 2014

On the Upside

Although end-of-life issues have been on my mind lately, I'd rather concentrate on being alive. Since "Life is like a roll of toilet paper—it goes faster at the end," I'm scrambling to fit everything in.

Right now, health-related commitments are competing with what I'd prefer to do. So far in October, I've had a flu shot and a bone-density test. Coming up, the dentist, a hearing checkup (what'd you say?) and a mammogram. No fun.

But on the upside, the instructor of my Jefferson class is in love with his subject and so knowledgeable about it that he is a great teacher. My music professor is brilliant and funny and is teaching me to listen to music in a whole new way. My Rembrandt class is going to the Museum of Fine Arts where we will see prints and drawings that only can be seen by appointment. My two non-profit consulting projects are teaching me things I didn't even know I wanted to learn. And my work with students applying to college is allowing me to stay in touch with young people, one of my favorite demographics.

For the first time since I retired, I am feeling overwhelmed by all that is on my plate.

How great is that!

December 28, 2014

Learning in Retirement

Fifteen months ago, I retired from a career I loved. I had expected a period of "adjustment" and I wasn't disappointed. In fact, I had a lot of trouble with not rushing off to work every morning. But after a bit of trial and error, I found a good balance of activities.

This fall, things got even better. I discovered that there is a whole new world of learning to explore in retirement. I'm listening to music in a new way because of an undergraduate course I audited. With fellow retirees, I studied Rembrandt's drawings in a six-week course and spent twelve weeks exploring the many facets of Thomas Jefferson. And I am watching the "digitization" of our world from a new perspective, thanks to a six-week course examining the effects of technology on our lives.

In retirement courses there are no pre-requisites The homework is manageable and there are no grades.

What's not to love?

March 5, 2015

Interview

The other day I was interviewed by an 80-something Professor of Management Emerita (I love that word) at MIT who's involved in a research study on retirement. (I am struck by the number of academics who propose research projects on retirement just when they are considering retiring. But I digress...)

The questions she asked me were on point. Did I retire because I was tired of my job? *No.* Was I pushed out? *No.* Why did I leave? *Because I knew I would never want to leave a job I loved so much, and it would never be "easy" to leave. Plus, I was 75.* How did I manage the transition? *Not so well.* Am I happy with what I am doing now? *Yes, I have a full life with a variety of satisfying activities.*

And then I answered a question she didn't ask. As happy as I am, as satisfying as the things I am doing are, nothing has replaced the joy of working for thirty-three years for an organization whose mission resonated so completely with me.

May 17, 2015

Moving On

Although it now seems like ancient history, my transition from the job I loved for so many years wasn't an easy one. At first, I avoided most of my former colleagues. I needed time to separate. Once I found my new rhythm, it was easier to be with them.

But the real test came the other night at a reception and dinner to honor the School's dean who was going back to teaching after eleven years of exemplary leadership. People came from near and far to pay tribute. Prominent invitees who couldn't make it delivered their words of appreciation by video on two huge screens. The dean's daughters spoke. His colleagues spoke. Big donors spoke.

I chatted with alumni, faculty, administrative colleagues and friends. Former deans hugged me, current faculty hugged me. The whole event was joyful, and I had a wonderful time.

More important, it was a "been there, done that" moment. I have moved on.

September 29, 2016

To Be One's Best Self

For the last six months, I have been coaching a young woman who works for a non-profit. Its CEO recognized her leadership potential and thought that outside coaching might be helpful.

I accepted the assignment as a volunteer.

We met every three weeks and stayed in touch by email in between. Our "office" was a quiet coffee shop in Harvard Square or, when the weather was good, a park bench. One time we met at her workplace because I wanted to see it.

We worked on her ability to manage up and manage down. We discussed her career trajectory. We strategized about whatever was on her mind.

Last week, our six months were up. At our last meeting, we talked about the progress she had made. I was delighted to hear that she is getting a big promotion, and that they have asked for her help in defining the job they are creating for her.

I don't take credit for making that happen. I do take credit for helping her become more planful about her future. In the note she handed me as we parted, she thanked me for helping her to reflect on what she can do to become her best self.

The funny thing is that I think I gained as much or from our time together as she did. Maybe more...

6

TAKING CARE

WELL-BEING

"Take care of your body It's the only place you have to live in."
Jim Rohn

I've never been a big fan of my own body. I was a way-too-tall female for my generation and pretty awkward. Eventually, I got more comfortable with who I was and how I looked. Although I am slim and in good shape, time has taken its toll. Still, when we hold each other in bed, my husband Peter tells me how much he loves my body. This is the only good thing about his failing eyesight.

It's been years since I started putting my index fingers on my cheekbones and pushing upwards to make my wrinkles disappear temporarily. Even longer since I bought my last bikini. But when I turned 70, other than a shift in gravity, most notably in my bosom, I still felt my body was OK.

Then, all of a sudden, it wasn't.

When I was 72, our grandson Grady, age four, asked me why I have a neck like a skeleton. When his mother had me try a moisturizer that she liked, Grady's older brother Leo remarked, "You do look less wrinkly Grammy." Less wrinkly?

I saw the light about the importance of exercise when I turned 40–which seemed pretty old back then. I began to run.

My go-to running outfit was a yellow Mickey-Mouse T-shirt, skimpy blue running shorts and a pale blue Bill Rogers running jacket. I visualized my mother turning over in her grave at the thought of my running. She got her exercise from moving mahjong tiles in her weekly game. But then she also never owned a pair of bluejeans.

Jane Fonda's exercise tape became part of my routine in my late forties. Her workout became my workout. And the workout of my closest neighbors. Three of us met twice-weekly to "feel the burn" and to catch up on the latest gossip. We were a neighborhood coffee klatch without the coffee.

The one exercise I always loved was biking. I remember feeling so fit when I biked four miles round trip to pick up the newspaper while on vacation at the beach with our kids. Then in my late 40's, we took our first real biking vacation. On that first trip to Provence in southern France, our son Jeremy, thirteen could barely fight the strong Mistral wind. The following year, we couldn't keep up with him. We had found our travel sweet spot and we never looked back.

For 25 years, we saw much more of the world from our bicycle seats than we would have from cars or trains. And at home, except when the temperature dipped to 25 degrees or below, I rode my bike to work every day until I retired at age 75. Even a knee-replacement at age 69 only kept me off my bicycle for six weeks.

My hair, like my Mom's, turned silver early and my hairdresser told me that people pay her to color their hair with silver streaks like mine. But now, there's much less black and much more white. And it's thinner. When I went to the beautiful parlor as a child, Phil, my mother's hairdresser, would get out the thinning shears. Alas, no more.

My body has its imperfections at 70-something (as it always has), but I recognize that things can and will go downhill. I am waging a battle against osteoporosis. And I stand on one foot when I brush my teeth in the morning and the other at night in the hope that good balance will save me from a bone-breaking fall. There is a laundry list of bad diseases that I have managed to avoid thus far. I eat well, am fanatic about exercise and try to get enough sleep. That's about all I can control. The rest is luck.

ROUTINE MAINTENANCE

For the majority of my life, "routine maintenance" meant taking my car in for regular checkups. No more. Now routine maintenance means doing whatever I can to prevent further deterioration of Judy Kugel AND the car. I am aware that for me, it's a losing battle. It is all about putting off the inevitable, but I'm giving it my best.

My maintenance program began at age forty when I decided it was time for my first facial. I wasn't convinced that it did much, but it sure felt good. At about the same time, I took up running. Running was not a popular female activity then. I know this because my first pair of running shoes was purchased on the men's side of the sporting goods store.

Rather than log the history of my increasing efforts to stay in shape, let's see where I am 30 years later.

I spend approximately nine hours a week exercising. Included are a 45-minute-weekday early morning session split between the elliptical trainer, the stationery bicycle and stretching. Add in a three times per week weight-lifting session, biking to and from work except in horrible weather, and an aerobic walk or two on the weekends. My reward comes when I refuse help in loading my carry-on into the overhead rack on a plane or a seat offer on the subway.

OK, occasionally I do take the seat. Seventy may be the new fifty, but not necessarily 24/7.

INSOMNIA

In the middle of the night, the slightest headache is an incipient brain tumor, a child not-heard-from has been abducted, a work concern is a full-blown crisis, and I'll never have an idea for another blog entry.

In the morning...all is well.

March 21, 2008

Knee Birthday

For years, I watched hemlines go up and down and more or less tried to keep up with the trend, despite my belief that fashion designers were out to get me to replace my wardrobe every season.

Recently, however, I have become less concerned with where my skirts end than I am about the knees they cover. Let's just say that I no longer take my knees for granted. I used to run, play tennis, and hike. That is until my knees started to hurt. In my late fifties, I had two arthroscopies to clean up torn cartilage, and substituted aerobic walking for tennis and running. Occasional short-term physical therapy kept me going until fourteen months ago when my knee had deteriorated enough that my orthopedist recommended a knee replacement.

Next week my new knee will be one year old. I've pretty much forgotten the brutal rehabilitation and the swelling that kept me in sweatpants for two weeks. I no longer hate the physical therapist and the woman who came to take my blood. I do take pride in a speedy recovery that allowed me to bike to work five weeks after surgery, much to everyone's surprise.

But it is only now, one year later that my new knee is down to the size of my old one. And although I hear a click with each step and am subjected to a body search every time I fly, I am grateful for the surgery.

I don't pay much attention to hemlines these days. My closet is full of pants.

March 25, 2008

Pain

A friend just returned from a safari in South Africa. She told me that although she had heard wonderful reports of similar trips from others, she never appreciated their stories until she experienced it herself. I feel the same way about sciatica. Until you experience the debilitating pain it brings, you can't imagine how it feels.

I'm usually pretty tolerant of pain, coming off pain killers after surgery sooner than most, for example. But sciatica was only a word to me until yesterday when I felt pain unlike any I'd had before. Gnawing deep pain, radiating from my lower back down the back of my leg. Unstoppable with Ibruprofen or Tylenol, waking me in the middle of the night several times.

Today I tried denial, my usual tactic when I'm not feeling well, but I was not able to tame this monster. So tomorrow I'm going to start dealing with the health care system.

What a pain!

March 18, 2008

ME AT 5X

My dermatologist has a very good sense of humor, I look forward to our annual "visits". Often he's been on a wonderful trip to India or some other exotic place so he is both entertaining and interesting.

He does not have a cure for my aging skin, however. Unlike the magazines I read at the beauty salon that promise me skin like a baby if I try one of the expensive creams and lotions they advertise, he only reminds me to use sunscreen and gives me samples of the latest SPF60 version.

Normally, I follow his advice.

But I didn't take him seriously enough when he recommended that I never look into a 5X magnifying mirror. Perhaps I bought one because I thought it would compensate for the inevitable deterioration of my up-close vision. Who knows? But morning and night I peer into its reflection to look for new lines or wrinkles. They never ease in. They appear suddenly in their full glory. And they look back at me almost triumphantly. It's kind of a "gotcha" experience.

For relief from this self-inflicted torture, I could turn the mirror to its non-magnifying side. With a flick of my wrist, I could see my face as others see it. But I don't.

August 14, 2008

OH NO, NOT ANOTHER ONE

I noticed it last night while brushing my teeth, but I hoped it was just because I was tired. After seven solid hours of sleep, I could no longer pretend it might be something else.

Yes, I have a new wrinkle. Actually, it's about three new little lines, horizontally across the bridge of my nose. They appear to have been the result of a stealth attack.

A variety of creams, plenty of drinking water, and the daily use of 30 SPF sunscreen, even in the winter, have been part of my wrinkle prevention arsenal for years. But I know that I am fighting a losing battle.

I guess worse things could happen…and they will.

March 8, 2009

CATARACTS

My cataracts are gone. Both of them. The second one was easier than the first—maybe because I knew the routine. But I am sure that I had less local anesthesia this time because I heard every word uttered in my short stay in the operating room. The topic was the chimp that ripped off the face of its owner's friend. What a cheerful subject to hear while under the knife so-to-speak! I could also hear the quiet whirring of the ultrasound machine breaking up my cataract. I could hear the surgeon saying "beautiful."

So I write 48 hours post-surgery on a computer screen that is whiter than it used to be, and I am not wearing glasses. I have lots of drops to take for quite a while—they are already a part of my routine.

Everything is a different, brighter color. And now that I see him better, I can report that Peter is even more handsome than I remembered.

May 28, 2009

CLL DIAGNOSIS

At my annual checkup last November, my internist noted a slight irregularity in my blood numbers. He suggested that we test my blood again in six months. I made a note in my calendar and forgot about it.

In mid-May, I repeated the blood test. This time my internist sent the results to a hematologist. And now I have a diagnosis of CLL or chronic lymphocytic leukemia, a condition in which your body produces too many white blood cells. There is a huge range of possible outcomes. According to my hematologist, who is now a very important person in my life, some people live for years with this condition. But not everyone.

It turns out that I have probably had it for a long time. A blood test from 1996 showed too many white cells, and my count is really no worse now than then. That is good news. I also don't have any other types of white cells that are irregular or any swollen lymph glands. That is also good news.

I will have to have my blood tested twice a year and my lymph nodes once a year. Although I have what could become a serious condition, I have just a speck of it, or as the hematologist called it "Stage Zero". I am not worried, but given the choice, I would prefer not to have it at all.

It's just six days since I received this news, and I am almost done processing it. Soon it will be just one more thing to be factored into my very good and lucky life.

July, 16, 2009

ENOUGH!

I try to be good about processing news that I'd rather not get. So when I received a diagnosis of CLL in late May, with its potential for turning to lymphoma in the future, (It could be very far in the future.) I worked at not dwelling on something I couldn't do anything about. Now there are days when CLL doesn't enter my mind at all.

At the time of my diagnosis, my internist told me I should see an endocrinologist, but I wasn>t sure why until yesterday when I had the appointment. Sure enough, I have yet another condition that showed up in my blood work. It seems that my parathyroid is producing too much of something that (to simplify it greatly) is stealing calcium from my bones. The condition is hyperparathyroidism, and the only cure for it is surgery. Not right now, but at some point yet to be determined.

Enough!

I know that more health issues come after you turn 70, but I spend more than ten hours a week exercising like mad to ward off disease and this is the thanks I get?

I'm now in my processing mode.

November 19, 2009

No If's, Ands or Butts

I have been thinking a lot about butts lately as part of assessing my aging body. (I'm tempted to say that I've tried to put all of this behind me.)

In ancient times, i.e., my father's era, the saying "I'd like to have that swing on my back porch" was not uncommon. But swings and back porches are pretty rare nowadays, as is that comment. More recently, my half-sister who is ninety-one speaking of her rear told me that she often has the feeling that someone is following her, and then "I realize it's actually me."

I've always had an ample rear end, but lately I've noticed that it seems to have flattened out. I turned to Google for answers. If you search for "aging butts," you get 7, 810,000 hits. I only looked at two. One confirmed that this phenomenon happens to all females of a certain age. The other showed before and after pictures of women, some as young as their early twenties, who have had butt lifts.

Who knew?

December 10, 2009

SURGERY

I'm in good health for someone edging up to age 72, and most of the time, I am just plain grateful to be here.

But even with an incredibly able surgeon in a top-ranked hospital, and a not-so-dangerous operation, I was not a happy camper as I waited for my parathyroid surgery last Thursday. Except during a couple of pre-op appointments, I had managed to avoid thinking about this unwelcome event until I left work the evening before. I told my assistant, Margaret, that I couldn't wait to see her again. For her, the next day would be normal. Not for me.

Over the years, I have had a handful of successful surgeries for fairly generic things like acute appendicitis and a knee replacement. I am good at recovering. But still, surgery is surgery, and it is never guaranteed that nothing will go wrong.

I find that once I am alone in the hospital, I retreat into my own zone. It's just me, the doctors and the nurses. I am completely in their hands. I don't think about anything except getting through the surgery. I know I will feel worse when I leave the hospital than when I came in, but I just hope to leave on my own two feet.

And I did feel worse when I left the hospital eight hours later. A sore throat from the breathing tube, stiff neck from the surgery, and lightheadedness from the anesthesia.

Now, a week later, I'm back to not thinking about my parathyroid. I've checked surgery off the "to do" list, and I am ready to move on to the next challenge.

Hopefully, it won't be in a hospital.

December 20, 2009

C IS FOR COLONOSCOPY

I try to focus on the good things about growing older, but I can't think of anything positive to say about a colonoscopy. I don't know what I was thinking when I scheduled it so close to Christmas. Maybe I thought that work would be quieting down and that I could skip a day at the office without missing much.

I didn't remember that my healthy diet would be turned upside down for five days. (Didn't it used to be three days?) It seems that everything that is good to eat is verboten. What's worse is that at holiday parties, foods with nuts and seeds and other forbidden ingredients prevail.

I haven't had canned peaches since I was a kid, but at least yogurt with canned peaches is better than yogurt without. That was my pre-C lunch for four days. On the fifth (or liquid-diet) day, lunch was my first-ever glass of Gatorade which actually isn't all that bad.

But can't someone invent a colonoscopy preparation that doesn't taste so awful? Or that doesn't make you shiver?

It's all behind me now—so-to-speak. And miracle of miracles, no polyps—which means I get to go five years before I repeat all this fun.

I do admire the nurses and doctors who respond to us grumpy, starving colonoscopy patients with a cheerful outlook and lots of warm blankets.

They deserve a Merry Christmas.

January 24, 2010

My Body

I feel great. Most of the time, nothing hurts. Yet lately I have begun to feel that my body is letting me down. I received a diagnosis of chronic lymphocytic leukemia last May. Even though it is "Stage Zero," it has to be watched. In August I found out that I had a growth on my parathyroid that was preventing calcium from being absorbed by my bones. That resulted in (successful) surgery to remove an adenoma (benign tumor) in early December. Ten days later I had a colonoscopy, and since a few adenomous polyps were removed. I have to be watched carefully and have another colonoscopy in three years, rather than the normal five to ten years.

It struck me that, body-wise, things are going in only one direction and it's the wrong one. As a friend who has had breast cancer put it, sometimes you feel like a walking time bomb.

What can I do? I already exercise rigorously. I try to limit the amount of red meat I eat. I pack in the fruits and vegetables. I (usually) manage stress well. I (usually) get enough sleep. I am aware that luck has a lot to do with what happens.

But that doesn't stop me from feeling like a walking time bomb on occasion.

February 28, 2010

THINNING HAIR

When I was a child, I had long thick pigtails. Then one summer, when we were visiting my cousins in Buffalo, my mother and aunt decided that I had outgrown them. Still braided, they cut them off. Just like that. My mother kept them in a manila envelope in the dining room buffet for years, I guess trying to keep a piece of her little girl.

Mother had her own beautiful prematurely gray hair cut at Phil's Beauty Salon in Pittsburgh where I grew up. She took me there for haircuts too. Phil had to use thinning shears on my very thick dark hair and I recall heaps of my hair being swept away by his assistant.

Years later, on vacation with Peter, and having just learned that I was pregnant, I was astonished and alarmed by the amount of hair left in the sink when I combed it in our hotel room in San Francisco. Hormonal change in pregnancy can cause hair loss, explained my obstetrician. But although my hair never reached its previous thickness after Seth was born, I still had more than enough.

Until recently.

Now, when I blow my hair dry, it seems to take less time. When I asked Kelly, who has been cutting my hair for twenty years if she noticed any change, she said that my hair is becoming finer, i.e., thinner.

Another trauma at 70-something!

April 4, 2010

TUMMY

On Friday I wore a pair of black and white "tweedy" pants and a short, chic black jacket to work. It's a spring outfit, and it was just right for a beautiful spring day of meetings. While I was sitting in one of those meetings, I looked down and noticed my tummy. I wear a size six, and I exercise and eat right. In all honesty, I've been known to gain a pound or two over the winter because I hate the short days. But I've never "noticed" my tummy before. I sat up a little straighter, but that didn't help.

It's true that Peter and I having learned how good dark chocolate is for our health, have been eating two squares just about every night for months.

On Saturday morning, I dug the scale out of the closet and weighed myself. As usual after the winter, I'm about two pounds over my preferred weight, but that's no different than in past springs. So what's with this tummy thing?

Maybe I need to go down to one square of chocolate and double the number of sit-ups I do. But I have this sinking feeling in my gut that it has something to do with…being 70-something.

September 12, 2010

MAKEUP AND ME (A HISTORY)

I've never been big on makeup. I'm married to a man who has been known to want to take his thumbs to women's eyelids when they are heavy with eye shadow. So my policy has always been "subtle."

Young skin doesn't need a lot of cover up. But I do recall the first day I wore makeup to work. I don't remember the exact date, but it was twenty-some years ago.

Back then, and for many years thereafter, once I had a hint of a tan, I happily took the summer off from makeup. But a couple of summers ago, I had to stop those makeup time-outs at work because sunscreen was effectively preventing any tan.

However, I was still able to hold out on weekends year-round, at least during the day. I didn't think the checkout person at the supermarket or the shoemaker cared about my pale complexion.

All of that changed yesterday morning when I looked into the mirror before leaving to run some errands. I didn't like what looked back at me. So, I picked up the tube of tinted moisturizer. Not for the checkout person, not for Peter.

For me.

June 9, 2011

CLL Year Two

On Tuesday I had my annual appointment with my hematologist. It has been two years since my diagnosis of chronic lymphocemic leukemia. CLL is a form of cancer in which increasing abnormal blood cells push out normal blood cells. Eventually, it becomes difficult to fight off infections.

There is no cure for this disease, but it can be treated. It's all about the numbers. So, twice a year, my blood is tested, and once a year, I see my hematologist who looks for increased numbers of abnormal cells and swollen lymph glands and asks about night sweats and other symptoms

About 363 days of the year, I don't think about my CLL. Thinking about it doesn't change anything, and there is nothing I can do to stop it. But when I have my semi-annual blood test, and when I see the doctor, I am reminded that I do have cancer.

Walking back to the car after my appointment, I felt sad. My numbers are a bit worse (they don't go the other way), but not alarming. Still, I wish that I didn't have this disease.

We had friends over for dinner that night. We sat outside in the garden. It was a gorgeous evening.

I felt better.

October 16, 2011

Puffy Eyes

A while ago, I decided to do something about my newly-puffy eyes. I headed to the cosmetics department of my favorite department store and asked for help from the perfectly-made-up saleswoman. She had *the* cream for me—a dab under each eye morning and night and no more bags, she promised. She said that no one had ever returned it. So I handed over way too much money and was on my way.

Seven weeks later to the day, I returned to the counter to spoil the record of no returns. I had a long conversation with a different saleslady. She said she lived by that cream, that if I had used it properly and it hadn't worked, I probably needed plastic surgery.

I told her I was seventy-three and since my husband's eyesight is failing, surgery seemed extreme. She said that I couldn't be seventy-three (I was wearing my tight Brazilian jeans). Then she told me that having survived breast cancer surgery fifteen years ago, she would never elect a surgical procedure. I told her I was glad she was still alive. Then I bought everything I could think of–lipstick, eye shadow, mascara. By the time I left, I had a new friend.

Now I have a new plan. According to the Internet, top models fix puffy eyes with cucumber slices.

Next stop, the produce department.

October 6, 2013

Make-up Exam

When I was a child, my mother's bedroom bureau featured a mirrored tray containing perfume bottles of all shapes and sizes. My father never had to worry about a Valentine's Day gift—perfume was the default. I loved pulling out the stoppers on the bottles of Chanel #5, Shalimar, Joy, or White Shoulders, imagining myself as a perfumed beauty with dark flowing hair, clad in a low-cut gown.

Alas, I married a man who hates perfume. And he's pretty anti-make-up too. He tells me that when he sees heavily eye-shadowed eyes, he is tempted to place a thumb on each eyelid and rub it out.

All this was fine with me when my skin was young and smooth and the only dark spots on my face were a side effect of my birth-control pills. But there came a time when, after my summer tan faded, my winter pallor required a little help–shall we say a tinted moisturizer and some blush?

Eventually the tinted moisturizer became as much a year-round necessity as the bright red lipstick that is my trademark. But I use eye shadow sparingly.

For obvious reasons.

July 24, 2014

The Upper-Arm Jiggle

I am compulsive about lifting weights. Therefore you would expect my biceps to be well toned. And so would I.

I hadn't given a lot of thought to the "buffiness" of my upper arms until my friend Kathleen mentioned over lunch last week that she now only buys T-shirts with sleeves that almost reach her elbows.

That evening, I spent some time contemplating my upper arms in front of a full-length mirror. I could see a bit of drooping skin when I held my arms a certain way. And it's true that I could make it jiggle (a little).

So I decided to do some in-depth research (aka Google) where I learned that if you can pinch an inch from the inside of your upper arm while in push-up position, you have a jiggling problem. I am relieved to report that I could only pinch a half an inch.

Nevertheless, I will keep an eye on my upper arms. I have a lot of sleeveless tops in my closet.

August 21, 2014

Nails, Hair, Youth

It was my Sunday night ritual for years. I would settle into the family room sofa to watch TV with Peter and the kids. And I would manicure my nails, usually with a fire engine red polish.

When a friend asked me where I had my nails done, I loved telling her that my manicurist was me.

Out with that very friend the other night, I was bemoaning the state of my nails. Maybe it's my celiac disease that robbed them of their strength. Or maybe just being older. My nails are always breaking and they are full of ridges. I keep them well filed and hope nobody notices.

In that same conversation, I was bemoaning the state of my hair. It used to be so thick that my hairdresser had to use a thinning shears. No more.

So, my beautifully manicured nails, and my thick tresses are gone. As is my youth.

August 31, 2014

My Doctor and Me

Like most people my age, I have some health challenges, but I like to celebrate how great I feel. You never know when that might change.

Like it did the Sunday night almost ten years ago when I felt a sharp pain in my abdomen as I got up from the sofa to go to bed. It came on me so suddenly that I decided to call urgent care at my health plan. The nurse told me to come in first thing in the morning, but since my regular doctor was away, she made me an appointment with a Dr. Bauer. Of course she told me that if the pain intensified, I should go to the emergency room.

In the morning, I dressed for work, expecting to be a little late, but moments into my appointment, Dr. Bauer sent me to the hospital for what turned out to be emergency surgery for my about-to-burst appendix. I was so grateful that I wrote him a thank you note and asked if he would become my primary care physician. He agreed.

Since then, he has been my savior on several occasions–like the time he identified a lump on my parathyroid and sent me off to a specialist for crucial and successful surgery. Or when he was worried about the result of a routine blood test and sent me to a hematologist who has managed my Chronic Lymphocytic Leukemia for the past five years. Almost a year ago when I struggled with retiring, he prescribed medication to help me sleep and called me regularly to see how I was doing.

On Friday, he retired.

In the spring, when he wrote to his patients to announce that he had decided to retire, I immediately replied, telling him that he couldn't do that. He's younger than I am. How could he retire?

When I saw him for my annual checkup last month, we had a great conversation about retirement and the future. And then we said good-bye.

Before I left, Dr. Bauer helped me choose a new doctor. I am sure she will be terrific. But it won't be the same.

November 2, 2014

The Shot that Fell Short

Years ago, Peter and I participated in a shingles vaccine study. We didn't know whether we had been given the real vaccine or a placebo. When it was found effective, the study directors contacted those of us who had gotten the placebo and invited us to be the first to get the vaccine. Peter had gotten the real stuff; I had to get inoculated.

So when I noticed a painful bite-like rash near my scalp after going to the movies a few weeks ago, I decided that there had been some spiders in the movie theater. A few days later, because the rash was spreading and more painful, I made an appointment with my dermatologist. Then a friend told me that she thought the rash looked like shingles. "Of course not," I said. "I got the vaccine."

By then, I was feeling pretty awful and since my dermatologist appointment was a couple of days away, I went to my primary care doctor who confirmed my friend's suspicion.

Because the outbreak was close to my eye, I had to see an opthamologist immediately because ocular shingles can damage your eyes. Fortunately, although my eye was nearly swollen shut, my shingles had not spread that far.

Now, three weeks later, I am much better. My rash is less angry and I have finished the anti-viral medication that made me feel worse, not better. My head still aches, but not so badly.

Bottom line: Get the vaccine, and remember that not all spider bites are from spiders.

December 14, 2014

FEAR OF FALLING

Falling has been in the news lately. Or maybe I'm just noticing it. Seven years ago, I fell and broke my hip. I remember how upset I was in the emergency room when the doctor told me that it was highly likely that I wouldn't be alive in a year. It is true that a broken hip is often the beginning of a quick deterioration, but that is not what you want to hear in an emergency room.

Anyhow, I'm still here.

But all this news about stumbling has not fallen on deaf ears. I find that I am paying more attention as I walk along the uneven Cambridge sidewalks. I try to remember to use the railing when I go up and down stairs. My balance is quite good and I do weight-bearing exercise to keep it that way, but I still pay attention.

Yet, the other day I did something foolish. My foot was asleep when I got up from the sofa. Rather than shake it awake, I put my weight on it. It buckled and as a result I had a swollen and painful ankle for about two weeks, despite my icing and elevating it. It could have been worse.

Just another reminder that now, more than ever, caution is required.

May 17, 2015

POSTURE

I was the tallest girl in my high school class. My mother was always reminding me to stand up straight. "SB," she would whisper, her not-so- gentle reminder to hold my Shoulders Back.

Now, years later, I have figured out that my rounded shoulders are partly genetic, but also partly the result of my trying to hide the fact that I was taller than most of the boys in my high school class.

I'm still trying to improve my posture. I think it's good for my health among other things. So the other day I asked Peter if he would gently remind me to correct my posture when he sees me slumping.

He responded by saying he doesn't nag. Wonder what that implied?

August 6, 2015

A(nother) Bullet Dodged

Things can change in a millisecond. But at 70-something, they seem to change way too often. In the last few months, two close friends (plus Peter) have tripped on uneven sidewalks and mashed their faces. No permanent damage, but a reminder that our balance isn't what it used to be, and we need to pay close attention. Every second.

When my dermatologist discovered something suspicious on my face in early July and told me that she was 90% sure that it wasn't skin cancer, but would biopsy it anyway, I didn't give it a second thought.

Until she called me while we were on our road trip to say that it was a basal cell carcinoma that needed to be removed. She quickly told me that the cure rate was very good and that there was no hurry as it was small and would grow slowly.

Sixteen days later, I had Mohs surgery by a skilled surgeon who was pleased with the outcome. Besides some restrictions on what I could do for ten days and an unsightly bandage on my face, I seemed to have dodged a(nother) bullet.

August 20, 2015

Goodbye to my Dermatologist

I just had my last appointment with my dermatologist. She is moving on to a teaching position in another part of the state. I've written before about her perfect complexion and sunny disposition. She's also one good doctor who examines every mole like it's the Hope diamond.

I asked Peter who was also her patient if he wanted me to wish her well on his behalf.

"Yes", he replied. "Tell her I'm sorry our relationship was only skin deep."

September 27, 2015

DOCTOR SEASON

My annual doctor appointments are clustered in the fall. It just happens to work out that way. But two appointments the day after Labor Day? What was I thinking?

8:30 a.m: to my ophthalmologist, a tiny powerhouse of a woman. Since my cataract surgery several years ago, she checks my eyes annually. The good news is all is well; the less good news in that I have aging spots on my retina that we have to watch. She also recommended using eye drops for my dry eyes and urged me to see my optometrist to be sure my glasses are just right.

1:30 p.m: to meet my new internist for my annual checkup. She grilled me on all my habits (mostly good) and pronounced me healthy. However, I've lost two inches of height and she is worried about my bone strength negatively affecting my spine. So I have to see an endocrinologist who may prescribe a dreaded-by-me osteoporosis drug.

I'm lucky to have good and caring doctors in this era of corporate healthcare. But how did two appointments turn into four? Maybe it's because I'm 70-something.

October 22, 2015

BUILDING BODY AND VOCABULARY

Normally, I wear a loose T-shirt and black exercise capris when Kathy, our trainer, comes to our house. But on Saturday I wore my body-clinging-sleeveless-scooped-neck exercise top (and black exercise capris).

I eagerly showed Kathy my "wall angels" because I've worked hard on them and have really improved. Her comment? "Judy, you have ripped deltoids!!"

She was stunned by the puzzled look on my face. She explained that "ripped" means high muscle-definition. In other words, I am very cool (for an old lady). She added that "jacked" is another word for having well-developed muscles. Improved vocabulary is just one more reason to keep exercising.

October 29, 2015

INSOMNIA AGAIN

When I toss-and-turn a couple of nights in a row, I try to figure out what's going on that's keeping me up.

Was it because I talked to my high school friend who had just looked at an attractive assisted-living community? She and her husband are healthy and still love their home of forty-plus years, but their kids don't live near enough to look after them and are worried.

Is it time for us to look?

Or was it because our furnace stopped working on that same bitter cold day? We have a service contract, but the gas company outsourced repairs to another organization. Rather than promptly sending out a technician, that organization told us that they couldn't send someone until the following week and offered to give us the names of some plumbers to call, promising to reimburse us for the expense. Except none of those plumbers could come that day either.

And finally, there is the possibility that I was worrying about our kids. This is a frequent source of sleeplessness. It seems both of them are working way too hard with no let-up in sight.

Maybe it was none of the above. Still, I'm tired.

December 20, 2015

BODY CHECK AGAIN

Although I am a fanatic exerciser, a healthy eater and do whatever I can to stay "young," the inevitable seems to keep happening and this time the inevitable is arthritis. Sure, my once-broken hip is a bit arthritic, but this was a front-and-center-overnight-appearing swelling of the first joint of my right index finger. It doesn't hurt; it just bulges.

Then there is my newly-discovered-dry-eye problem. Counter-intuitively, when your eyes tear excessively, it means you have dry eyes. On a scale of ten, if ten is very dry, my eyes are an eleven, according to my ophthalmologist. If the wind whispers, my eyes weep. If it's below sixty degrees when I am riding my bike, tears roll down my face. Now, a tiny bottle of fake tears accompanies me wherever I go. I'm new at this so chances are about 50-50 that I'll actually get the drops in my eyes five times a day.

And have I mentioned that the veins in my hands are much more prominent? Did you know that "vain" ladies hold their forearms up to hide this? Try it.

All these are reminders that time marches on. And luckily, so do I.

March, 20, 2016

My Old New Knee

My replaced right knee is having its ninth birthday next week. I barely remember the painful and seemingly slow recovery from that surgery. I do recall that my surgeon was not happy about how quickly I got back on my bicycle. I had to promise that I wouldn't go up any steep hills for a while.

Now, I only think of that surgery on its birthday or on the rare occasions when I notice the six-inch scar on my knee.

But I do remember enough not to want to go through it again. So when I feel a twinge in my other knee, I tell Kathy, our trainer and she adds exercises to strengthen it.

Like me, knee replacements don't last forever. Like me, so far so good.

March 27, 2016

It's Getting Harder

I start every weekday with my self-improvement hour or maybe I should call it my "fighting-off-the-inevitable" hour. (Others might call it "exercise".) I have been doing this ever since I stopped running twenty years ago.

But I'm finding it harder to resist the smell of coffee and the awaiting newspaper in the morning just so I can live longer.

Forcing myself to exercise is not the only thing that's getting harder. Although I can still get up from the sofa easily, it takes me a few steps to get my body lined up correctly. And in museums I find myself looking for a place to sit down sooner than I used to.

I wouldn't even try a once-easy fifty-mile bike ride, and I regret that and lots of other things I can no longer do.

On the other hand, there are so many things I can do. And that's what matters.

March 31, 2016

Bragging

Kathy, our wonderful trainer, came to our house last Saturday for the first time in almost four months. She is so good at what she does and she has an amazingly positive attitude toward life. She loves us and we love her.

She worked with Peter on his balance for quite a while.

When it was my turn, Kathy asked to see my push-ups. I did fifteen in what she said was perfect form. She told me that plenty of people her age (forty) can't do that. She insisted that I brag about it on the 70-something blog. She said that it might inspire others to work on staying in good shape.

I do whatever Kathy tells me to do.

June 5, 2016

Bat Wings

Put this in the category of "Now I've heard everything!" According to *The New York Times*, it will soon be possible for doctors to use hyaluronic fillers to fix upper-arm skin that hangs like bat wings. (If you don't know what hyaluronic fillers are, you probably haven't worried much about those ever-deepening facial lines left by a lifetime of smiles.)

As a vigilant observer of my own increasingly imperfect body, I rushed to the mirror, took off my shirt, and had a look. Alas, it's true. The skin on my upper arms isn't as tight as it once was. But bat wings? Not yet.

I will continue lifting weights because I think exercise slows down the inevitable. But for a solution that's easier (and cheaper) than hyaluronic fillers, I think I'll just stick with long sleeves.

September 11, 2016

ANNUAL CHECKUP

Oh for the days of short annual checkups that ended with my doctor telling me: "You're healthy as a horse." Not sure exactly what that meant, but since there were no referrals or follow-up appointments, I could assume that all was well.

No longer. My checkup on Thursday lasted more than an hour, partly because my doctor is thorough, but also because there seem to be more things to check these days. And as usual lately, there is follow up– "Let's do an X-ray to see if your hip pain is arthritis, bursitis or something else", she said.

She also suggested a blood test for vitamin B-12, not included in my pre-appointment blood tests just ten days ago. That blood test had left me with a huge black-and-blue bruise. So this time I asked the technician to be extra careful. She offered to use a "butterfly needle"—thinner and less likely to produce a bruise, she promised.

Ten minutes later, I took a peek. Alas, there was another big bruise. And to add to the fun, this time my bandage was soaked with blood.

It's good that annual checkups happen only once a year.

September 18, 2016

ANNUAL CHECKUP PART II

Several very good friends, over the years have been diagnosed with breast cancer. Thankfully, (sometimes after very difficult treatments) they are fine for now.

So I remained calm when my doctor told me, during my annual physical last week, that she wanted me to have a diagnostic mammogram because she felt a suspicious thickness in my left breast. A "diagnostic" mammogram consists of the usual exam with extra pictures of the area in question plus a sonogram.

I went on with my life as usual, but began to feel anxious on the day of the exam. The technician promised me that I would get the results immediately either way. The mammogram itself was long and painful. The technician showed no reaction to the pictures, which is the right thing for her to do.

The sonogram seemed to take forever. Back and forth and back and forth over the same spot. No emotion on the technician's face. After what seemed like forever, she finished and left me to get the radiologist. During her long absence, I was thinking about how I would deal with a breast cancer diagnosis.

The radiologist wanted to look for himself. So, more gloop, more back and forth with the sonogram transducer.

Finally, the result.

"You have very dense tissue, but we see no malignancy," said the radiologist.

Phew!

8

KEEPING UP

═══════

TECHNOLOGY

"Technology is a useful servant, but a dangerous master."
Christian Lous Lange

In 1965, Intel co-founder Gordon Moore correctly predicted that the number of transistors that would fit on a chip would approximately double every two years, a theory still known as Moore's Law. Translated for technophobes, that means things electronic have progressed like wildfire, and that's why our smartphones are so smart, so small and so fast. Within the next few years, those in the know anticipate that there will be a slow down of the doubling, thank goodness.

When I think about what the breakthroughs of my childhood were–TV for one–I can't imagine what my parents would think if they could have a peek at our electronic devices today. Nor can I imagine what I might think of technology forty years from now. Surely, self-driving cars will be common. There will be daily package deliveries by drone, implanted chips that monitor our vital systems, and who knows what else?

June 22, 2008

The Cell Phone Challenge

My husband Peter has a cellphone. On his cellphone are a number of unread messages. Fewer than there used to be because he never retrieves his messages and I've stopped leaving them. Our children gave up long ago.

Here's the problem: Peter carries his phone with him, but only turns it on when he needs to make a call! I have explained ad nauseum that if I needed him in an emergency, I would be unable to reach him.

I thought I was the only one with this problem. But a young colleague of mine says her mother does the same thing. When Margaret had a flat tire not too far from her mother's house, her mother didn't have her cellphone on, causing much inconvenience and dismay to her daughter.

Another colleague related that her elderly aunt's grandchildren insisted that she get an answering machine and bought it for her. She had my colleague come and record the message for her. It said, "You have reached so-and-so. You can leave a message, but I won't call you back."

So much for technology.

August 10, 2008

Ridge Road, A Dramatic Documentary

It was 1989. We lived on Ridge Road a great neighborhood with plenty of friends for our kids. But that summer, a key Ridge Road family was moving away. Our boys and a friend decided to make a video of the neighborhood as a going away gift. They borrowed a video camera (think one grade above the home movies of the 1950's). It was bulky and unreliable, but they managed to interview all of the neighbors without breaking the camera. Considering the technology and the experience of the producers (none), it was funny and moving and some of its classic lines are still in our repertoire, e.g., "Mmm Mmm Mmm, smells like a barbecue".

Technology changes, so a few years ago, fearing the VCR technology would disappear, I had the video made into a DVD so that we would have a copy for posterity. But when YouTube came along, our children decided that everyone who lived on Ridge Road back then should have a chance to see (a much edited) version of "Ridge Road: A Dramatic Documentary" on the Internet, 19 years after it was produced.

They introduced the condensed version on YouTube as follows:

"The Rowe family moves to New York City, ripping a hole in the fabric of a utopian corner of 1980s Boston suburbia. Three young filmmakers with virtually no talent (but dashing good looks and keen fashion sense) capture the moment."

November 2, 2008

KEEPING UP

I resisted Facebook as long as I could. I finally "joined" because my son Jeremy set up a page for me when I wasn't looking. I must admit that Facebook is actually quite good, and although I don't report my daily activities, I do occasionally check on what my 51 "friends" are up to. (Friend-wise, Jeremy is way ahead of me at 450, but this is not a contest.)

As for a "smart phone", I was determined never to join those rude people who read their email on their Blackberries when they think I am not looking. The amount of time I spend on my email at work is frightening, not to mention that I already check it on my home computer on nights and weekends. So I drew the line—no Blackberry for me.

Alas, my boss finally insisted that I be reachable 24/7 via email. And so I now have a two-week old Blackberry. I have not begun to explore all the things it can do. Just thinking about that gives me a headache. But while waiting for planes in several airports last week, I have to admit it was kind of fun to be connected.

Thankfully, I don't have an iPod, and I don't have Tivo. Yet.

November 20, 2008

Blackberry Update

My new Blackberry is five weeks old today. Because I have been critical of other people's use of their "smart phones," I'm a bit embarrassed to report that I am loving mine. Instead of having to cram a Palm Pilot and a phone into my handbag, I have this slick 3.9 oz. item that does all the things they both did plus lets me deal with my email and browse the Internet. No longer do I have to stand idly in line in the supermarket or twiddle my thumbs if I'm the first person to a meeting. No longer do I have to run upstairs to check email at home.

Of course, there is a learning curve for new users, and I have had to call the Verizon help line a couple of times with my questions. And although I'm not as speedy as the next generation, my aging thumbs are already typing away reasonably fast.

I heard that President-elect Obama will have to forego his Blackberry because his email messages would not be secure and they would not be saved for posterity (or investigations). I sympathize with his distress.

Yesterday, I replied to an email from our son Seth with my Blackberry. He responded immediately with the following message, "Love the Blackberry—you're so modern."

Modern? Yes. Also addicted.

November 8, 2009

Technology in Primavera, Brazil & Silver Spring, Maryland

Our son Seth, the Brazil correspondent for Globalpost.com wrote from the town of Primavera this week. He went to the Amazon, away from his usual post in Sao Paulo, to check out education in Brazil's biggest state (Amazonas). He will be writing about how education works in a region where there are few roads, and kids go to school by boat

From Primavera this week, he wrote about the town's electrical system. When there is gas for the generator, everyone watches soaps and/or soccer on the town's few TV sets

More than 3,000 miles away and in a different hemisphere, his brother Jeremy launched a web business this week. I think the idea came to him and his friend about a month ago, and it's up on the Web already. He didn't have to worry about a generator. Jasmere.com will offer discounts of up to 70% from specialty web businesses—it's a shopping site, with a different angle. If you like bargains, you might want to sign up.

How unbelievable is it that two brothers are 3000 miles apart yet the news from both this week is about technology. Two very different technologies.

September 19, 2010

TECHNOLOGY (CON'T)

Although I frequently vow that I am in the de-accessing stage of my life, technology still seduces me.

In the past month, we have purchased:

1. An internet radio, that lets us hear a station anywhere that streams over the internet.

2. A new printer, not because ours didn't work, but because the new one is better.

3. A Roku Digital Video Player that let us access our Netflix queue on our TV instantly and remembers where we were if we have to stop in the middle to answer the phone.

4. A netbook. This handy little device for internet and email is so convenient that it sits (barely noticed) in the kitchen and has eliminated the constant yelling back and forth up and down our stairs—"Are you almost off the computer?"

So the other night when Peter reported that several students in his new class had iPads and told me all the cool things about them, I declared ENOUGH.

Someone has to draw the line.

January 16, 2011

Home Delivery

I have a new worry. I am afraid that one of these days the newspaper will stop being delivered to my door. I don't know what Peter and I will do without a newspaper at breakfast. We could bring laptops to the table and read online, but that wouldn't be the same. Plus, we only have one laptop.

It isn't that we don't have anything to say at breakfast. But we talk about what we are reading. To be specific, one of us reads what's interesting in their section of the paper out loud even though, of course, the other person will have that section soon.

A couple of weeks ago, I was reading that a Danish shipping company is paying $2.4 billion to a *South Korean* energy company to acquire its *Brazilian* pre-salt oil deposits assets (whatever that means). I read it to Peter, observing that it was a great example of our "flat world".

There was also a story about how badly Britain was handling an inch of snow in Essex. It seems that there was a car accident that injured a passenger. An ambulance came to take him to the hospital. The ambulance crashed on the way to the hospital, and the guy was killed. All because of an inch of snow!

Peter then reported that James Franco, the lead in the movie *127 Hours*, enrolled in four graduate programs simultaneously after his BA, one each in film, writing and poetry and one leading to a PhD in English. He's published a book and currently has a solo art show in a New York gallery.

I could survive without coffee or my favorite granola at breakfast time, if I had to. But please, please don't take away my morning paper.

April 7, 2011

What Sherry Says

It's hard to pick up a newspaper these days without finding an article about the declining use of telephone conversations and the rise of texting. The average teenager is said to send/receive about three thousand text messages per month. Just the other day, a friend told me about a local teenager who was sitting on the living room sofa next to her best friend. Perhaps three feet apart, they were texting each other.

I was dumbfounded.

MIT professor Sherry Turkle, who has written extensively about the effects of computers on our lives, describes this kind of behavior in her latest book, *Alone Together: Why We Expect More From Technology and Less From Each Other.*

She reports that:

1. There is a growing tendency to text rather than talk.

2. Online, we perform. Our Facebook page is not who we really are.

3. We are never "alone", and therefore, we are in danger of losing our capacity for solitude.

I took an hour out of my workday to attend a talk by Professor Turkle. When she described her Thanksgiving dinner last November, she admitted that although relatives had flown in from far away, they all had their handheld devices on the table during the meal.

I found her talk fascinating. However, that didn't stop me from glancing down at my Blackberry. Like her Thanksgiving guests, I was unable to disconnect.

July 17, 2011

Technology (con't)

Our Yahoo mail provider recently asked us to upgrade (free) to its new and improved version of email. That was not surprising. What was surprising was that they thanked us for being with them for *eleven* years. It seems like only yesterday when our son Jeremy set up our Yahoo account and suggested the password that we still use.

We had had email at work for a few years by then, but we still talked on our landline phone to colleagues and friends and even hand-wrote an occasional letter.

I don't remember what year we got our first cell phone. I do remember it was big and that we left it in the glove compartment of our car for emergency use only.

I do remember that on a business trip to Mexico City in 1999, I was astonished that everyone there used cell phones. I decided that cell phones must be a necessity because the traffic in Mexico City was so horrendous that people needed phones to let each other know how late they would be.

Technology has been on my mind since we walked past a McDonald's on Sunday. There was a woman outside the restaurant.

She was having a lively conversation.

On a *pay phone!*

March 14, 2013

Reply to All

From time to time, I think about the difference technology has made in my life. Usually I think of it positively, like when our son calls us from Brazil using Skype and it's free. Or when we "visit" our grandchildren via our iPad and watch what they are up to at that very moment.

I depend on Google as my encyclopedia. I use the web as my restaurant-finder and movie reviewer and weather.com to see how warmly to dress. And just yesterday, I ripped a dusty, yellowed-paper list of phone #'s from my bulletin board at work because my computer has more current info.

Peter and I think the "lady" on our GPS has saved our marriage. I have loved my BlackBerry for years, although I may have to switch my allegiance to the iPhone's Siri, when she improves her batting average.

But when someone emails our book group to ask if we are attending the monthly meeting, and people REPLY TO ALL, that's another story. I can wait until the meeting to know if Mary or Sue is attending. Then, there are those at work (You know who you are!) who always REPLY TO ALL. It takes a nanosecond to decide who needs to see your reply.

Give the rest of us a break.

November 14, 2013

Google Maps

Peter and I are lucky to live a short walk from our country's first garden cemetery. Cambridge's Mount Auburn Cemetery was founded in 1831 and is now a National Historic Landmark. Its seventy-five acres attract residents of Greater Boston and visitors from around the world for bird and plant watching.

Wandering its winding pathways, we discover new monuments and plants each time we visit. In the spring and summer the flowering trees and shrubs are beautiful. In the fall, the foliage is breathtaking. Even in winter, Mount Auburn's 5,5000 varieties of trees, shrubs and other plants covered with snow are a photographer's dream.

During our walk there on a crystal clear Veteran's Day, Peter was taking pictures for his photography class. I pulled my phone out of my pocket and took a picture of him taking pictures.

Just for the fun of it, I opened Google Maps on the phone, wondering if it could find us on Acacia, the tiny path we were walking. Sure enough, we were spotted. We decided to let Google Maps guide us home, and as the time to our destination kept changing, we realized that we didn't walk as fast as it expected us to. But when we got to our house, sure enough the phone announced that we were there. And immediately, a picture of our house appeared on the screen.

Amazing, but a little scary…

December 5, 2013

Glympse

The pre-Thanksgiving storm forecast for the eastern seaboard had me imagining the worst. Our kids normally beat the traffic by leaving at 2:00 a.m. on Wednesday morning, driving eight hours straight and arriving on our doorstep by 10:00 a.m. As a certified worrier, I pictured fog, multi-car pile-ups and worse.

But thanks to Glympse, an app on my smartphone, I was able to see where they were and how fast they were moving at any moment. From the time I woke up until they walked in the door, kids still in their p.j.'s and parents upbeat, I checked on them periodically. Seeing that arrow moving along the map on my cell phone was all I needed to know they were safe.

I can't help but think how it had been for my mother. When I was little, my father was a salesman, on the road from Monday through Friday. My mother told us that if she opened the front door on Friday night at 5:00 p.m., Dad was probably pulling into our driveway. If not, she wouldn't have a clue about where he was.

Things have changed.

April 17, 2014

Is the Internet our Friend?

Last week's news about the Heartbleed Bug, a major Internet security breach, convinced me to change my passwords.

I started with my Yahoo Mail. I had used the same password forever and I liked it. Changing it was a pain. But it got worse when, after changing the password on my computer, I tried to check my email on my phone. I got the following message: "Cannot reach server." I had to delete my Yahoo account from my phone and re-install it with the new password, a reminder that technology is not always our friend.

Except when it is.

For example, this past weekend our Maryland kids/grandkids made a last-minute decision to drive to Philadelphia. It was the grandkids' spring break so there were no football or soccer games to miss. We learned about it from a texted picture of our grandchildren in front of the Liberty Bell with the caption "Guess where we are."

They called Sunday night to describe their adventure. Jeremy had decided to try his new college alumni phone app that tells you if any alums are nearby. Jeremy opened it as they neared Philadelphia only to find that a good friend from his freshman dormitory lived ten minutes away. He clicked on the name, got a phone number and called. The friend was at home with his wife and two sons the same age as our grandchildren. They had a three-hour reunion.

Meanwhile, Katrina posted the Liberty Bell picture on Facebook. A good friend of hers who lives half-way across the country sent an email saying "About to fly to Phillie and would love to see you." So she and Katrina were able to meet for a catch-up coffee.

Gotta love the Internet. But like many things in life, we have to take the bad with the good.

May 18, 2014

BOOMER TECH

I have no idea why the *Washington Post* invited me to a presentation on Boomers and Technology. I'm not even a boomer. But I am always up for the latest technology news. So I decided to go. I figured there was a 50-50 chance that I'd like it.

It was wonderful. There was a great series of panels. Here are some of their messages;

From MIT Agelab Director, Joseph Coughlin: Older folks embrace technology if it is fun. It's fine that toilets can now tell us how healthfully we are eating and what we weigh. And that stoves can tell us that we forgot to turn them off. But what we will love is technology that allows us to continue to drive, to live longer and better, technology that allows us to have fun.

From the Entreprenuership Panel: You don't have to be young to be an entrepreneur. In fact, you improve the more you do it, claimed Bill Aulet, Managing Director, Center for MIT Entrepreneurship. He urged us to heed the advice of Gabriel Marquez "We don't lose our playfulness because we get old. We get old because we lose our playfulness."

Panelist Geri Brin, started faboverfifty (www.faboverfifty.com) to celebrate boomer women five years ago. Her site now attracts several hundred thousand visitors monthly. Visit it and be inspired. And Jeanne Sullivan, co-founder of StarVest Partners advised all would-be entrepreneurs to get a personal Board of Advisors to support their new undertakings. And then she offered her card to anyone who wanted help.

The Tech for Life Panel showed us innovations for managing fitness and health. And much more.

I had to take my bike, a subway and a bus to get to Boomer Tech, but I'm delighted that I did.

August14, 2014

WHO'S CALLING?

It's been quite a while since we bought our answering machine that announces loud and (not-so) clear who is calling. We've gotten used to not picking up the phone when it announces "not-a-vale-a-bill" or "private caller." The latter is most often an appeal for a charity or a vote. It's not that we don't give or vote. We just prefer not being called at dinner.

We do pick up "cell phone MA" because I don't recognize all our friends' cell phone numbers, but we can be sure when it's "cell phone TN," where we know no one, that it's a solicitation.

When our son Seth was in town the other day, he wondered why we didn't answer when "PrintLink" called, but picked up Parkinson, Barbara whom we don't know. Hearing "Parkinson" announced when your father has Parkinson's disease is a bit unsettling, but when it turns out that it is your brother calling, it's really strange. What Seth didn't know is that Jeremy's phone is a work phone, formerly belonging to one Barbara Parkinson. We've gotten used to it.

But when I heard my cousin Joanie's message later, I remembered that her husband's firm is Printlink, and I was annoyed that I had missed her call.

Although we are unusual in having a landline at all, we are unique in having a *son* who is announced as "Call from Parkinson, Barbara."

September 21, 2014

A VISIT TO OUR LP'S

Remember long-playing records? That's how we used to listen to music. When Peter and I got married and put our records together, we had quite a collection–classical, popular, show tunes, jazz.

Remember CD's? That's how *we* listen to music now. But for most people, the way to go is some form of streaming music. As usual, we are behind.

Last weekend, we paid our annual visit to our records. They reside in the New Hampshire vacation home of our friends Gordon and Christa who still have a record player, just like the one I owned fifty years ago. We listened to some of our favorites as we always do.

I told them that our son Seth had said that LP's are coming back and that we shouldn't have given away our collection. The next thing we knew, all of our records were in our car. Well, all but a few that Gordon and Christa really like. And they still have a couple of hundred from their own collection and donations from other friends.

Of course, we don't have a record player, but Seth says he will buy one. So, he will have our record collection and we will continue to visit them in their new home.

We are holding on to our CD's.

April 30, 2015

FACEBOOK FRENZY

I have 144 friends on Facebook. (I just checked.) I have no idea where they all came from. I only know that I have never asked anyone to be my friend, so they must have asked me. Who knew?

Although some of my "friends" post every day, I rarely do. However, on Sunday, when Peter and Seth (home for a one-day visit) and I went for a neighborhood walk, we passed a gorgeous blooming tree, and Seth took a selfie. I thought it was Facebook-worthy. I posted it at 7:30 pm.

Before I knew it, there were 53 "likes" and 9 comments. Since Seth has 1609 friends (I just checked), I thought most likes and comments would be his, but 21 likes and 5 comments were my friends. Like I said, who knew?

April 28, 2016

MEN DON'T ASK

It's not news that men don't like to ask for help. Before the advent of GPS and Google Maps, getting Peter to ask for directions at a gas station when we were lost was an exercise in futility. I get it. It's a male thing.

So when we were looking for alternatives to cable because our bills were skyrocketing, I was the one who asked for help from our neighbor Jean who, unlike other octogenarians, doesn't have to ask ten-year-olds how to work her electronic devices. Jean had happily canceled cable. I asked her how she managed without it.

Jean invited us to her home for a demonstration of cable-free options, and we followed her advice. The other day, when she came over for a thank-you glass of wine, she mentioned that she watches shows she enjoyed on cable via YouTube.

Good idea we thought. So Peter tried but couldn't figure out how to get it. At my suggestion, he reluctantly emailed Jean and, of course, she had the simple answer we needed. So now we have YouTube on our TV.

Will men ever learn that it's OK to ask for help?

Doubt it.

October 2, 2016

LANDLINE-LESS AT LAST

We canceled our cable TV a couple of months ago because we were tired of paying for a million channels that we never watched. Best decision ever.

That is until we canceled our landline phone. Maybe it was the endless political robocalls. Or maybe we heard from one too many charitable organizations. For sure, we were hearing from too many "Name Unavailable" callers. Our phone rang from dawn to dark and we couldn't stand it any longer.

It's been an amazing change. We are celebrating the silence. Of course, cell phones are not immune to robot-calling so I'm not sure our celebrating will be long-lived.

But for now, we're loving it.

7

NOT BY BREAD ALONE

SUSTENANCE

"Everything in moderation…including moderation"
Julia Child

As a little girl, I waited by the oven while my mother's apple pies were baking. She always managed to have a little extra crust that she would dust with cinnamon and sugar and put in the oven just for me. It was my favorite "cookie." My brother would come home from school and grab some iceberg lettuce from the fridge that he would slather with mother's homemade thousand island dressing. (Oh, the things we remember!)

Peter and I both like to cook. Soon after we met, he made me dinner at his apartment. I was impressed that his copy of Julia Child's "Mastering the Art of French Cooking" looked more used than mine. (Of course, later I learned that it wasn't that it was used so much. Rather, he tends to spill stuff on cookbooks.)

The food I am the most loyal to is coffee ice cream, so it appears in several blog entries. And the meal I love the most is Thanksgiving. No gifts, just family together. It's the only thing that makes November bearable.

Thanksgiving, always a favorite day, is somehow more poignant lately because we can never take for granted that we will all be together next year. But at 70-something, I am grateful for every day, whether or not it ends with coffee ice cream.

January 21, 2008

Coffee Ice Cream

I've always been a purist when it comes to ice cream. No goppy chocolate sauce with peanuts and whipped cream for me. Just give me the real stuff.

For as long as I can remember ice cream has always been my comfort food. From the 5-cent Creamsicles and Fudgicles of my childhood to the super-high-butter fat premium ice cream in my freezer today, I just can't resist my favorite dessert.

For my birthday in my sophomore year in college, my friends made a scavenger hunt for me. Each clue led to a spot in our dorm that had a gift certificate for a pint of ice cream. I remember feeling so ill from overeating one of those pints of ice cream that I literally stuck a spoon down my throat. I'll skip the details.

Today, my portions are more reasonable and I rarely indulge more than once a day. During the workweek, ice cream is allowed only every other night. But it has to be premium. It has to be coffee. And it has to be Starbucks.

October 5, 2008

I've Got the Celiac Blues

When I opened the refrigerator door this morning, I saw three loaves of special breads–artisan whole wheat, raisin, and seeded whole grain. They are made by companies with wonderful names like When Pigs Fly and Nashoba Brook Bakery. They are delicious, I am told, but I can never eat a single bite of them.

Almost nine years ago, I was diagnosed with an auto-immune disease I had never heard of, celiac sprue. I cannot eat anything with gluten, ever. And gluten lurks in anything with wheat, barley and rye, most soy sauce, beer and most cereals. It isn't just that I would have an allergic reaction, but gluten does bad stuff to celiacs' intestines over time that can lead to life-threatening diseases. It's not pretty.

It was bad enough to have to give up my morning bagel, but there are

166

worse things. When we are invited to dinner with friends, I have to remind them of my eating restrictions. When they served just-baked-chocolate chip cookies the size of saucers at work meetings, I have to pass. When we go to restaurants, I have to call in advance to make sure they can accommodate my diet and still worry that someone will drop a bread crumb on my plate.

On the plus side, more people are being diagnosed with this disease. And therefore, there are more gluten-free products available online or in stores. And restaurants are paying more attention to allergies. At home I eat wonderful meals. I didn't have to give up coffee ice cream. So it's not all bad, and it is getting better.

Nevertheless, some days I feel depressed about being gluten-intolerant. It doesn't make me feel better that others have worse afflictions. Seeing those loaves of bread this morning made this one of those days.

I've got the celiac blues.

November 26, 2008

Thanksgiving—the Prequel

This morning when I woke up, all my most-loved ones were in my house. This only happens once a year. So I savor every moment.

I thought I was the first person to get up, so I quietly headed down to the basement to do my morning exercises. It turned out that our younger son Jeremy was already up, and he decided to join me. Normally, my companion is the newspaper. This morning, it was Jeremy and I chatting away, he on the elliptical trainer and me on the stationery bicycle as if we did this all the time. A very precious thirty minutes.

When we came up, everyone but Seth was awake and at the breakfast table—the grandkids with their specially-bought sweetened (but not too sweet) cereals, and the rest of us grabbing various parts of the newspapers along with whatever our normal breakfast is. The noise at breakfast, not too common around here when it's just Peter and me, is a delightful change.

The day flies by; the kids go out to see friends they've know since elementary school, 25 years ago. Grady, the younger of our two grandsons, naps when they return and we have some quiet time with his older brother. There are a lot of conversations that are extensions of the hurried telephone chats we have while the kids are busy in their own lives.

We have a glass of wine before dinner, and I anticipate a day of cooking and eating too much tomorrow. I love every minute of it.

November 30, 2008

THANKSGIVING—THE SEQUEL

The cranberry-orange sauce was in its usual white soufflé dish, the turkey on the used once a year wedding-gift platter. All the traditional foods on their usual serving dishes.

It's Thanksgiving Day at our house.

The time-worn recipe cards had been on the kitchen counter for days—what could be made ahead was in the refrigerator or freezer. The size, time and temperature of cooking of all of our turkeys have been duly recorded on the roasted turkey page (235) of "From Julia Child's Kitchen" annually since 1987. The sizes ranged from 14 – 24 lbs. Once again the calculation was made. This year's bird at 14.95 lbs was done right on schedule after 3.5 hours.

Thanksgiving is a labor of love, and I get my reward as both of our boys fill their plates for the third time, and Seth proclaims it the best meal of the year.

I don't take Thanksgiving for granted any more. Each time that I see the next generation and the generation after that around our Thanksgiving table, I feel the passing of time, and I realize how grateful I am that we are all together once again.

November 25, 2009

THE FOURTH THURSDAY IN NOVEMBER

Tomorrow is Thanksgiving. We are all together. Seth has come from Brazil. Jeremy and his family have come from Maryland. These are the moments I cherish. When did I start worrying that each Thanksgiving could be the last we are all together? Of the last thirty-eight, there was only one that we weren't all together, and that was when Jeremy was living in Chile.

The house barely accommodates us all now that three year-old-Grady needs a real bed. The refrigerator is bursting at the seams because this group requires three different kinds of milk, dozens of cartons of yogurt, two dozen eggs, several kinds of juice and all the usual items. This is the one time of the year I miss the two ovens and two refrigerators of the house where the boys grew up.

November is a mean month. It's gray and damp and the last leaves have fallen. Spring seems so far away. Thanksgiving is the saving grace of this month, and, once again, we have so much to be grateful for.

Nov/ember 29, 2009

DOUGHNUTS AND LAPTOPS

Plus ça change, plus c'est la même chose. I don't usually rely on my rusty French, but somehow, "the more it changes, the more the more it's the same thing" sounds better in French, and this aptly describes Thanksgiving at our house. We don't vary the menu. Same great food, served in the same bowls and platters, the same branches of bittersweet gracefully surrounding the candles, the same last minute scrambling to make sure everything gets to the table hot.

Some things, however, do change because we change. We're all a year older, and it shows the most in the grandkids. When we went around the table to say what we are thankful for, almost-six-year-old Leo gave his thanks in Spanish and three-year-old Grady spoke in paragraphs rather than the two or three words strung together with his mother's help last year. The place cards, made on Thanksgiving morning by the kids, will grace all future Thanksgiving tables. For the first time I put fresh thyme in the stuffing, and it did not go un-noticed. So some things actually are different.

Around noon on Thanksgiving, with the turkey in the oven, we took our usual walk around the nearby reservoir, accompanied , as always, by a Nerf football. But this time, Leo and his dad decided to run ahead. We lost sight of them, and when they rejoined us, we realized that they had detoured to a just-off-the-path Dunkin' Donuts where they bought doughnuts and coffee for all. We sat on some rocks consuming multiple doughnuts as multiple passerbyers wondered why our family would be eating doughnuts right before turkey.

That was a change.

The other notable change came after the grandkids were in bed. Our three adult children, three open laptops, end of conversation.

January 17, 2010

COFFEE ICE CREAM REVISITED

This is not the first time I've written about coffee ice cream. It's my favorite food in the whole world, but only if it is made by Starbucks. When Starbucks ice cream disappeared from my grocery store over a year ago, I called the customer service number on a container I had in the freezer, and learned that the brand had been sold to Unilever, the huge conglomerate that owns Ben and Jerry's, Dove soap and just about everything else. Customer service told me that Unilever was going to use Starbuck's recipe.

It took a long time for Starbucks ice cream to reappear in the grocery store, and when it did, it was only in pints and the price had gone up 50%. So I rebelled and tried every other brand of coffee ice cream–Edy's, Friendly's, Brigham's–you name it, I tried it. Tonight, while not enjoying Friendly's mocha chip, I finally decided that I deserved better.

I announced to Peter that I was going to bite the bullet and go back to the Starbucks brand, no matter what the price.

After all, I am getting old. I need to make the most of every day.

November 14, 2010

HAPPINESS

In his famous 1943 paper, Abraham Maslow suggested that we have basic needs such as food and shelter. Once those needs have been met, we have psychological needs, self-actualization needs, etc. If you Google

Maslow Hierarchy of Needs, you will get about 4,530,000 results in 0.12 seconds and can learn much more about this.

My basic needs are quite well met. I am fed and sheltered. I have wonderful family and friends. All that is good. But lately, I've been thinking about what makes one day happier than another. For example, on Thursday, after an endless series of gloomy, damp, typical November days, the sun shone brilliantly. I could feel my happiness meter going up.

Clouds giving way to sun gives me a feeling of well-being.

The following also favorably affect my happiness score:

EVENT	POINTS
A really good night's sleep	10
A productive day at work	10
A call from one of our children	10
A call from one of our children who sounds happy	15
A dish of Starbuck's coffee ice cream	20

Professor Maslow would turn over in his grave if he heard that Starbuck's Coffee Ice Cream topped my hierarchy of needs.

November 24, 2010

THANKFUL JAR

Our daughter-in-law Katrina has started a new Thanksgiving tradition. Every day, she and Jeremy and our grandchildren, ages four and six, must write (or ask their mother to write) a different thing that they are grateful for. All of their notes go into the Thankful Jar.

Earlier this week the rest of the family were assigned the same task. We had to do a bit of catching up since they were already on day five by the time we got our instructions. At our Thanksgiving dinner, everyone will read their Thankful List. My list is very long.

November 27, 2011

TALKING TURKEY

Thanks to our daughter-in-law Katrina who suggested the tradition, we have a Thanksgiving Grateful Jar. Before digging into dessert, we read one another's notes that say what we are grateful for. We express our gratitude for each other, our homes and our health, and for Reese's peanut butter cups.

This year, however there was an additional pre-dessert reading by Seth who read a short article about Thanksgiving from the turkey's point of view. Not surprisingly, turkeys see this holiday differently than we do. The article was quite funny and no one laughed harder than Gramps (aka Peter).

Once we had quieted down, Seth announced that the article had appeared about sixty years ago in "The Maroon," the newspaper of Colgate University.

It had been written by a staff writer named Pete Kugel (aka Gramps).

April, 26, 2012

WHAT IS IT ABOUT COFFEE ICE CREAM?

I have been an ice cream fanatic for as long as I can remember. Just ask anyone who ever lived with me–my parents, college friends, roommates, and Peter, of course. And we're talking pure ice cream here. I am not a big fan of hot fudge sauce or whipped cream, although the dulce de leche topping we had in Argentina was something to write home about.

On my first trip to Europe in 1958 (back when we actually took pictures on film), my favorite photo was of a sign that said "ice cream" in five languages.

I've now survived more than a dozen years without gluten, but I'm not sure I would survive a week without ice cream.

Although I love all flavors of ice cream, I am partial to coffee. In fact, I order it 99% of the time. But of late, it has had a particular effect on me. It seems that when I finish my coffee ice cream, I cannot resist accosting Peter with my (clothed) form of lap dance. He doesn't seem to mind.

What is it about coffee ice cream?

November 25, 2012

Just a Week Ago

It's been a week since Thanksgiving. The guests' sheets and towels are back in the linen closet, the bed in the TV room is a sofa again, and Peter and I are back at our usual seats at a much-too-big dining room table. A pair of boots and a leather jacket left behind are the only visible evidence that we had guests.

Our grandchildren are back in their busy school lives; their parents back to their routines. Our travel-writer son is off skiing frugally (an oxymoron) in Vail.

I wrote the following email more as closure for me, but I include it here as my real farewell to Thanksgiving 2012.

"Children and grandchildren, Thank you for making the trip and for participating in my very favorite holiday with Gramps and me. I'm just getting used to the fact that you will not come bounding down (or up) the stairs with a big hug for us. PK and I have been saying how lucky we are to have such a great family--and we couldn't do it without you. :-)

Basically, we are proud of all of your accomplishments, all of your kindnesses to us, and all of the love I felt around the table, not just at Thanksgiving, but all week long. I want to do a special shout-out to Katrina for her non-complaining Tivo work.

We love you and are grateful for another Thanksgiving together, Grammy."

May 16, 2013

Gluten-free Mother's Day Weekend

I could write about how great it was to be with our son Jeremy and his family in Maryland for Mother's Day. I could say how amazing the grandchildren are, how much I enjoyed Leo's soccer game, the barbecue at their neighbor's, the visit with a childhood friend, our Mother's Day brunch, and Seth's Mother's Day email from Berlin which, of course, made me cry. All good.

Instead, I want to write about gluten.

We went to lunch after Leo's soccer game. The kids and Peter went to Five Guys, a hamburger place, and Katrina and I went to Sweetgreens next door where the counter staff composed a gluten-free salad per my direction, but put a piece of bread on top of the greens. "No," I shouted—you'll have to start over—I said I needed gluten-free."

"Not to worry", they replied. "It's gluten-free bread!"

We took our salads next door to join the males. Five Guys makes their French fries in a dedicated fryer and they are therefore gluten-free. I ate my first fast-food French fry since my celiac diagnosis fourteen years age. It was heavenly.

The one disappointment was at Costco's on Friday night where Peter and Jeremy each had a huge ice cream dipped in chocolate and crushed almonds. The woman at the counter didn't understand what gluten was so I couldn't join them. Peter admitted it was fantastic. I sulked.

But when Jeremy called Costco customer service after our Mother's Day Brunch and learned that, in fact, that bar is gluten-free, we took a quick detour on the way home, and Jeremy bought me my own ice cream bar dipped in chocolate and crushed almonds. Delicious.

Life is gluten-free and good.

April 19, 2015

SWEET ENDINGS

My love affair with coffee ice cream continues. With a gun to my head, I would choose cinnamon or coconut. But our freezer always has two quarts of coffee just in case.

I don't eat it every night since ice cream is not a healthy choice (although I plan to start daily consumption on my 80th birthday). But because I crave something sweet at the end of dinner, I have a couple of cookies on non-ice cream nights.

My favorite is a gluten-free oatmeal-raisin cookie that I buy from our trainer Kathy's mother-in-law. The trouble is that they are only sold in stores in New Hampshire, and I only get them once every other month when Kathy comes to our house.

I freeze a bunch and take out two at a time. I microwave them for thirty seconds. I eat them slowly, savoring each chewy bite. I finished my current supply yesterday.

I told Peter they are "the coffee ice cream of cookies."

November 26, 2015

GRATEFUL JAR

Early in November, our son Jeremy reminded us that it was time to start writing messages for our "grateful jar". Once more, we will pause before our Thanksgiving dessert and pass around our "jar", each of us picking a message to read until it is empty. I, of course, am completely emotional about all this. The other day just writing about why I'm grateful for Peter caused my eyes to fill with tears.

But this year, we have more to be thankful for than ever before. We live in a free country, and although we weep for those who were killed in terrorist attacks in the past few weeks, we are not confined to our homes like the people of Brussels or bravely sitting in a Paris café to prove that we are not going to let terrorists change the way we live. For those who lost loved ones, it has been dreadful.

In all of this sadness, I was touched by the young French father whose wife was killed and who spoke out about how he would not give the terrorists the gift of his hatred. Of his seventeen-month-old son, he said, "Every day of his life this little boy will insult you with his happiness and freedom because you don't have his hatred either."

Studies have shown that expressing gratitude is good for our health. We should be thankful every day, not just on Thanksgiving.

December 3, 2015

TRADITION

They arrive on Wednesday, the kids from Maryland at 9:30 a.m. after driving through the night; our New York son, late that evening. And this year there was an extra guest—Molly, the Maryland family's new dog.

The Thanksgiving dinner menu is always the same, although this year we added Brussels sprouts. The big difference of course is the kids. Our eleven-year old grandson is taller than I am and fills his uncle's shoes. His brother, just turned nine, did the heavy lifting when we set up the sofa bed for his uncle in the basement.

They tossed the football in the back yard, as always. A willing stranger took our annual Thanksgiving family picture when we paused in the middle of our while-the-turkey-is-in-the-oven-late-morning walk around the reservoir, as always. The Black Friday shopping happened (without the grandparents) and the kids went to a Boston Celtics basketball game in the evening. Seth's very entertaining high school friend Jon came for his usual dessert visit, but this time with his new fiancé.

We played *Wits and Wagers*, a great family game that our daughter-in-law had bought us with more guests on Saturday afternoon, and brought in pizza for dinner with still more guests on Saturday night. When Seth headed back to New York after dinner, it felt like he had just arrived.

The Maryland family got up in the middle of the night for its 3:00 a.m. Sunday departure, and I got up to say good-bye. It was only when I got back into bed that I realized that I had forgotten to send the last two pieces of French Silk pie home with them.

Another Thanksgiving, with all of its traditions, like clockwork, wrapped up.

December 24, 2015

BAGELS OR BUST

It's been sixteen years since my celiac-disease diagnosis meant no more gluten in my life. Decent gluten-free food was an oxymoron back then, but it's gotten better, and most restaurants can accommodate my diet today.

But no one, yes no one, has made a gluten-free bagel that remotely resembles what used to be my breakfast staple. Believe me, I've tried them all.

So imagine my delight when America's Test Kitchen's *How Can It Be Gluten-free, Volume II* claimed that after endless experimenting their cooks had developed a recipe for like-real bagels.

Last Friday was a gloomy day, good for a kitchen challenge. We had amassed the fifteen ingredients that our new recipe called for, including psyllium husks, oat flour, white rice flour, brown rice flour, xanthan gum, molasses, etc.

Peter and I were a team in the kitchen—he was captain, and I followed his orders. We used every conceivable bowl, pot, cookie sheet, measuring cup and utensil in the house. All kitchen surfaces were covered with gluten-free flour.

It was not pretty. For the first time in forty-seven years, I wondered if our marriage could survive. We did everything right—measuring the flour on a scale, boiling the bagels one at a time and turning them over in the boiling water after five seconds, carefully arranging them on two layers of cookie sheets over oiled parchment paper. And that was only part of the drill.

When our six bagels finally went into the oven, we agreed that this wasn't meant for a home kitchen, and even if they turned out to be divine, we'd never make them again.

I managed not to try one until Saturday morning. Lo and behold, they were chewy and dense. I felt like I was eating something that wasn't just air. I can't remember real bagels all that well, but I was mightily impressed.

Will we do it again? No way.

8

ON THE ROAD

TRAVEL

"I haven't been everywhere, but it's on my list."
Susan Sontag

Travel is high on my list of life-long-joys, and I have been to almost fifty countries. From childhood fishing trips to the Muskoka Lakes region in Canada with my dad to two milestone-celebration-weeks in Zimbabwe and Botswana with our kids in 2000, seeing how others live has been one of my favorite things. Vacationing on our bikes was a 25-year tradition, but our five trips accompanying Seth, *The New York Times'* Frugal Traveler, were the most memorable of all our travels.

Today, traveling is more of a challenge—the airport hassles, the sardine-like seating on planes and our own declining stamina. But we're not done yet!

April 26, 2009

Children say the darndest things. They also live in the darndest places. That's why I write this from São Paulo, Brazil, third largest city in the world and a place not on my "see before I die" list.

Like everywhere else, it has its plusses and minuses. On the downside, the language is impossible to pronounce (at least for me), the city is huge and overwhelming, and it's a long trip from home. On the plus side, our son Seth is living here. That trumps everything.

Twenty-four hours into our visit, I am no longer overwhelmed. I am getting to know his neighborhood and the little café next door where this morning, my huge glass of fresh-squeezed orange juice was about a dollar. We've walked into the center of the city and visited the municipal market full of, among other things, exotic fruits that I happily sampled. At lunch near the market, I had a plateful of food from the buffet. The farofa, a grain-like Brazilian staple made from yuca flour and butter, was my favorite. It has a pleasing nutty flavor, and I'd be happy to have it be a staple in my home too.

São Paulo is for foodies. And for us as long as Seth is there.

May 3, 2009

This morning over a breakfast of guava juice and pão de queijo (cheese bread) in a juice bar near the apartment we rented in Rio, it seemed like we had come to know at least a small part of this great country that plays such a large part in our son's life.

Our road trip from São Paulo to Rio was a beautiful drive, mostly along Brazil's stunning coastline. We spent two days in the colonial town of Parati, including a trip to a "you can't get there from here" beach in Trindade, forty minutes away. We sat at a table on the beach in our bathing suits while eating one of the best meals (shrimp in a sauce made with dende oil) of our trip. We then drove to Rio where we spent two nights, had two great dinners, saw the city from the heights of Sugarloaf and

Santa Teresa, and walked for hours along Ipanema and Copacabana, two of the world's most famous beaches.

And suddenly it was time for us to leave Brazil.

It wasn't a perfect visit, but it was pretty darn good. It's hard on both sides when parents parachute into a grown child's life for eight days. But our visit got the job done—we can now picture him in his São Paulo apartment, and we know some of the places he hangs out. We have experienced the richness he sees in the Brazilian culture. We have seen the challenge and the opportunity that Brazil offers him.

Seth dropped us at the Rio airport for our 3:30 flight back to São Paulo and then to New York because he was heading north to Minas Gerais for work. By the time we boarded the plane, I had forgotten the few not-so-great moments of our visit. As the plane climbed into the sky over Rio, tears ran down my cheeks.

It never stops being hard to say good-bye to one's child.

June 28, 2009

Traveling with Friends

We've been traveling with our friends Christa and Gordon for twenty years and, except for a few days in Paris or Rome on our way somewhere else, we haven't been to the same place twice. Until this year.

We decided to return to the Hudson River Valley in New York State because we missed too much on our first visit. Gordon didn't have enough time at the Franklin Roosevelt Library in Hyde Park; we never got to nearby Eleanor Roosevelt's home or the Vanderbilt Estate. As for me, I had to go back to the Culinary Institute of America because they offered just-baked gluten-free bread. We had been on bicycles for our last visit, so this time we wanted to hike along the Hudson River. We also wanted to revisit the outdoor sculpture garden at the Storm King Art Center.

We managed to do it all in four days (although this required leaving Gordon on his own at the Roosevelt library while we went off hiking).

Our highlights:

The Culinary Institute of America: On a beautiful site overlooking the Hudson River, the campus includes three gourmet restaurants. Graduating students cook, serve and clean up under the supervision of their instructors. Many go on to become famous chefs. The head chef at McDonald's is a graduate.

Storm King: About a forty-minute drive south of Hyde Park on the other side of the Hudson, the Storm King Art Center is set on five hundred acres. The sculptures are by internationally-known masters. Maya Lin, whose Vietnam Memorial graces the Mall in Washington, DC, has a new installation called Waves, built on eleven acres that were formerly a gravel pit.

Any trip is even better when you share it with good friends. We like to travel with Gordon and Christa because we know them so well. We know that they usually sleep a bit later than we do. They always have coffee after dinner and we don't. If the rooms where we are staying are not equal, we flip a coin to decide who gets first choice. And wherever we go, we can count on Christa to find wild berries by the side of the road.

One great thing about being old is old friends.

January 28, 2010

A Dream Come True

I'm a push-over for animals in their natural habitats. There is something about peering into nature without disturbing it that gets me every time. I loved visiting Alaska, especially Denali National Park. Watching Mt. McKinley emerge from the clouds at sunset with a moose in the stream just behind me brought tears to my eyes. Three years later, I wept in the Johannesburg Airport at leaving behind the elephants, giraffes, and lions of Zimbabwe and Botswana.

And now I have returned from my dream vacation to the Galapagos Islands off the coast of Ecuador. Visiting there is a privilege. The giant tortoises, some over 100 years old, the baby sea lions and their mothers, and the blue-footed boobies doing their mating dance, are not afraid of us because they have no predators and visits by humans are limited.

Dolphins playfully dive near our ship. Iguanas are on almost every rock, flamingo's with their pink reflections in the gray lagoon feed at sunset. We snorkle with sea lions, turtles and assorted sizes, shapes and colors of fish.

A dozen of us and a naturalist in a zodiac, leave the ship for different adventures, a different surprise for each of seven days. White beaches, black beaches, even a green beach. Golden iguanas on land only. Marine iguanas black on one island, red and green on another. Islands "uplifting" from below or sinking to gradually disappear in a million years. Walking on what was once the sea floor.

When we took the final zodiac ride to shore for the flight back to the mainland, I watched our beautiful ship sparkling in the sunlight get smaller and smaller.

As usual, the tears came.

January 31, 2010

MACHU PICCHU

After a magical week in the Galapagos Islands, I expected an add-on to nearby Peru to be a letdown. But Machu Picchu had also been on my must-see list for years. And so we went.

Machu Picchu is "one of the new seven wonders of the world." An Inca city from the 15th century, abandoned by its inhabitants in the 16th century because of the Spanish conquests, it was in such an unlikely and hard to reach spot high in the Andes and so hidden by an overgrowth of vegetation that it was not fully re-discovered until 1911.

No list of "places to see before you die" would exclude Machu Picchu.

Since we were coming from sea level to 8000 feet, we spent a few days in the (lower) Sacred Valley of the Incas to adjust to the altitude. This is an agriculturally-rich area with farming both in the valley and on terraces built high into the mountains. The fields are still plowed by oxen. It was the rainy season so everything was lush and the green and iron-red mountains, part of the Andes, are "new" enough to present impressive ragged edges.

The village of Urumbamba and the nearby Inca fortress at Ollantaytamba were a good introduction to the savvy and strength of the Incas. From Ollantaytamba, it is an hour-and-a half-train ride through the valley to Aguas Calientes followed by a twenty minute bus ride on a narrow climbing road to the Machu Picchu site.

Words or photos cannot adequately capture Machu Picchu. It is a city of 80 acres that once had a population of several thousand people. The buildings left by the Incas are built of huge granite boulders fit together with precision to make temples and living quarters. We spent hours climbing up trails and among the terraces used to grow crops and through the remains of these buildings. The mist moved in and out among the peaks; the view changing from moment to moment.

The Incas of Machu Picchu worshipped the sun and moon and nature. Their stories have been mostly lost, but the power of their spirit is still there.

And it is very moving.

August 5, 2010

THE FRUGAL TRAVELER IN NICARAGUA

Nicaragua was never high on my list of countries to visit. To be honest, it wasn't even on my list.

But when our son Seth, aka *The New York Times'* Frugal Traveler, agreed to let us travel frugally with him in Nicaragua as part of his three-month Brazil to NYC assignment, the country became our most-desired destination and the country where we would spend a week I shall never forget.

Since Seth rarely knows where he is staying before he arrives, our only instructions were to meet him at the Managua airport's Budget Car rental parking lot sometime after 1:00 p.m. on July 28th. He was flying in that morning from Bogota, Colombia. We had flown from home the day before, and had spent the morning in Granada, a colonial town about an hour from the Managua airport, fairly incompetently getting around that attractive colonial city.

Because we had no way of contacting Seth, I imagined all kinds of things that could go wrong. But as we tried to ask the lady at the Budget counter where their cars were parked, I spied the Frugal Traveler squatting on the floor about ten yards away, computer open on his lap, planning the first day of our journey. In the short time since his plane landed, he had bought a Nicaragua phone chip, and was calling places in the northwest corner of the country where we might stay. He then called his credit card company to see what insurance they covered for the rental car, got some Nicaraguan cordobas, and was ready to roll before I could get over the fact that we had actually found him.

For six glorious days we watched Seth negotiate prices, directions, and keeping gluten out of his mother's meals. We watched him charm tour guides and taxi drivers. We came in way under our budget of $70 per person/per day including the price of the car. Although one place we stayed didn't have a bathroom ensuite, it made up for that by having great people and stunning sunsets over the Pacific.

Seth's Spanish is flawless, and that helped, but his commitment to mixing with the locals (and dogs) of all ages had us seeing the country in a way we could never have done on our own.

Most important, it was pure joy to have six days with an adult son who took such good care of us, while at the same time proving to us that we have not outgrown adventure.

Even at 70-something.

June 23, 2011

Croatia with Seth

When Seth told us that his summer assignment was to travel to countries on the coast of the Mediterranean, we asked if we could join him for a week. Although we had a great time with him in Nicaragua last summer, we weren't so sure he'd want to put up with his spunky, then old (and now a year older), parents again.

But he said he would and even allowed us to choose our country. We had wanted to visit the Dalmatian Coast for years, and seeing Croatia frugally was fine with us. So that's where we've been.

To say it was an adventure we will treasure is an understatement. Croatia's coast is a never-ending panoramic picture postcard. The Adriatic Sea is a palette of blues surrounded by hills/mountains that come down to its shore. You have to see it.

This area has a complicated history. You have to read it.

But the people have to be experienced, and that is easy to do in Croatia. In all of our travels, we have never met friendlier or more helpful people. We were treated like treasured guests by the people who rented us apartments or rooms in their homes and exactly the same way by people on the streets of Dubrovnik, and on the islands of Mjlet and Korčula.

Of course, the best part was being with Seth, watching his remarkable competence. He doesn't plan ahead much, so we didn't even know where we would go, or how we would get from place to place. Except, we knew it would be frugally.

We also didn't know that we would love Croatia.

We never see enough of Seth, so to have a solid seven days with him was a huge bonus. But it came with a price—saying good-bye without knowing when we will see him again. So, having just returned, I do feel a little sad. But more than anything, I am very grateful.

July 1, 2012

Norway Seth's Way

When Seth invited us to Norway for a week as part of his frugal summer in Scandinavia, we were thrilled. Although we joined him the last two summers, we would never take another invitation for granted.

Our trip started when we met Seth in Oslo and left on an eight-hour bus trip to Fjaerland where we spent two nights at a campground at the end of Norway's longest fjord. My book lay unread on my lap as we traveled through a countryside dotted with farming villages, snow-capped mountains, waterfalls, deep green hills, and grazing sheep, all under a cloudless sky.

Our trip ended with two nights on a sturdy old cruise ship sailing along the western Norwegian coast. It was the season of the midnight sun, and at midnight we joked that we couldn't tell if the sun was rising or setting. Peter and I had a cabin, but Seth slept in the lounge in true Frugal Traveler fashion.

In between, we visited Brønnøysund, Bergen, and Balestrand. We biked on the island of Vega, a UNESCO World Heritage Site where the friendly locals invited us to share in a festival marking the summer solstice, and a young woman named Ina opened the eider duck museum just for us because we arrived there after it closed. People were kind to us everywhere, partly because they were charmed by Seth, but mostly because they were just nice.

There were many unforgettable moments. One, in Brønnøysund when we were killing time waiting for the ferry to visit Vega, we came upon a choral competition in the center of town. We sat on benches and listened to groups from all over the area singing their hearts out. We had no idea what was going on, but we loved it.

At the campground where we stayed for our first two nights, Peter and I went for a walk after dinner while Seth wrote. It was about 9:00 p.m. The sun was shining on two houses high in the mountain, one a deep red and the other a dark mustard color, typical of the region. We went back to get Seth because it was such a beautiful scene. The three of us walked together, taking pictures of the mountain and of each other, a family without a care in the world.

Over coffee on our last morning together, we looked at the hundreds of photos of our week that Seth had downloaded to his computer and tears flowed (mine).

The trip itself was a dream come true, but what really mattered was the chance to watch Seth work, to laugh at his jokes, to have him laugh at some of ours, and just to share a piece of his life.

At our age, we realize that our best days may be behind us, but as our trip with Seth suggests, there can be some very good ones to come.

September 4, 2014

ART TRIATHLON

Williamstown, MA, located in the Berkshire Mountains close to the Vermont border, is home to Williams College. It is also home to the Clark Art Institute and the Williams College Museum of Art. Just minutes away in North Adams, the Massachusetts Museum of Contemporary Art (or Mass. MOCA) occupies a campus of old industrial buildings.

This summer the Clark finished a $100 million plus renovation that has put this "fusty" art museum back in the headlines. Williams College welcomed its students back with an exhibit of art they can borrow for their dorm rooms. And Mass MOCA, with its huge installations, featured Teresita Fernandez, a contemporary sculptor and artist in a breathtaking exhibit called As Above So Below.

We managed to visit all three museums over the Labor Day weekend. Of course, we didn't have the stamina to see everything, but once again I was grateful for my art history courses over fifty years ago.

Summer 2014 was beautiful in New England, perhaps to compensate us for our awful winter. As always, it went too fast. But spending the last weekend in a beautiful place with good art and dear friends–it doesn't get any better.

September 28, 2014

FRUGAL VANCOUVER

When Seth invited us to join him again for part of his annual Frugal Traveler summer trip, we couldn't refuse. Flying across Canada for four days with your grown child is a no-brainer.

However, this time there was a catch. *We* had to do the frugal planning for the "older generation" portion of his three-part Pacific Northwest trip. He gave us a budget and the rest was up to us. He would only go along.

That meant another challenge, one we put to ourselves. We had to be "better" than the younger generation planning the rest of his trip. We didn't want anyone outdoing us in providing frugal fun.

The planning was not easy. According to one source, Vancouver is the second most expensive city in the world (after Hong Kong). Peter and I spent hours on the Internet to find a place to stay and plan our days. We had a "had to do", "want to do", and "just too expensive" list of activities. We knew that we would be riding a lot of buses because our Airbnb accommodation was a ten-minute walk plus half-hour bus ride from downtown.

Peter did the bulk of the planning. My major contribution was to serve as trip cashier, holding all our Canadian cash. Funding innumerable bus rides, each requiring $6.25 in Canadian coins was a challenge, although most stores gave change with a smile.

Everything worked. The weather was perfect. The flowers, the mountains, the art, the neighborhoods, the "frugal" restaurants, our apartment in the 'burbs, the long walks, the togetherness with one of our (charming, handsome and talented) grown sons made for a way-too-short trip.

When Seth left us downtown to catch a train to Seattle, we had one more bus ride to our apartment. Without Seth, we only needed $3.50 in Canadian coins.

April 2, 2015

JEFFERSON AND FRIENDS

My 11th grade U.S. history book was grayish-green. It was big, and it was heavy and I have forgotten 99% of its contents.

But last week changed that. We were in Virginia because, in a class Peter and I took about Thomas Jefferson last semester, we were so impressed by this Renaissance man that we decided to visit Monticello.

Our five-day tour included visits to the homes of Presidents Madison and Monroe who were Jefferson's neighbors and friends. Our mornings consisted of lectures; our afternoons of visits to Montpelier, Ash Lawn-Highland and Monticello. Each place was lovingly restored, but Jefferson's Monticello won our best-in-show award.

Jefferson asked that his tombstone credit him only for the University of Virginia, The Virginia Statute for Religious Freedom and The Declaration of Independence–no mention of his presidency. Monroe, who served as Secretary of State and Secretary of War at the same time under Madison, never forgot that he was a soldier first and was referred to as Colonel Monroe until his death. Madison, our shortest president, wrote the model for the Constitution and the Bill of Rights.

Our next history visit will be to John Adam's home in Massachusetts. Although it's only thirty minutes away from our home, we've never been there.

So little time, so much history to re-learn.

May 3, 2015

Just a Subway Ride Away

The trip to Virginia that Peter and I took in March to visit the homes of three great American presidents was not a big deal for us, especially as compared to the many long overseas vacations we have been lucky enough to take.

What is a big deal is that we live a 30-minute subway ride away from the birthplace of our second and sixth presidents, John Adams and John Quincy Adams, and had never been there. To remedy that, we found a clear day on our calendars and penciled in a subway trip to Quincy, Massachusetts.

The birthplaces of the two presidents are just 75 feet apart and less than a mile from the Atlantic Ocean. The homes are old, by any standards, the first built around 1650.

We have come to expect excellent guides from the National Park Service, and we were not disappointed. After a quick visit to the original homes, we were "trolleyed" to the home that John and Abigail Adams purchased in 1788 after his years abroad as a diplomat.

Peace Field, set on 75 acres of former farmland is a "very Genteel Dwelling House." Everything in the home is original, including John Adams' standup desk, and his library of 10,000 books. The living room chairs that Adams bought for the White House and took with him when he returned to Massachusetts prompted a question from a visitor. "Why are some of the seat cushions so tall and others "normal"? Turns out, according to our guide, Krystal, that the thick-cushioned chairs were for the women. The taller pillows prevented the arms of their chairs from lifting their full skirts and revealing anything immodest.

It is pretty embarrassing to admit that we have lived in Massachusetts for over fifty years and had never visited the Adamses' homes. But when, a woman from Texas on our tour admitted that she'd never visited the Alamo, I felt better.

July 5, 2015

GETTING TO KNOW BOSTON—THE GREENWAY

What! We've lived in Boston for over fifty years and we've never been to (*fill-in-the-blank*).

Peter and I decided to make up for lost time. So after our visit to the homes of the two Adams presidents in nearby Quincy, we spent a beautiful Sunday afternoon doing the Beacon Hill Art and Garden Walk and, most recently, joined a guided horticultural tour of the Rose Fitzgerald Kennedy Greenway, built on top of Boston's infamous Big Dig.

Boston's Central Artery/Tunnel Project, aka "The Big Dig" buried the elevated highway between the city and its harbor. It was the most expensive highway project in U.S. history, costing approximately $24.3 billion and taking nearly forever.

The Greenway covers 15-acres, and has six distinct parks, each with its own personality. It has a series of organic gardens, lots of public art, a carousel and even food trucks. A Greenway Conservancy horticulturist, who shared his love for every plant and tree, led our walk.

The tour was free, but we came home and wrote a check to the Conservancy, in thanks for a wonderful morning.

Our "See Our Own City Initiative" is paying off.

September 6, 2015

GETTING AWAY

Planning a travel vacation at our age is risky, but our luck has held and we have just returned from a tour of eastern Europe that included a visit to Auschwitz in Poland, a four-hour hike through the splendor of the sixteen lakes and countless waterfalls of Plitvice Lakes National Park in northern Croatia, the crowded Charles Bridge in Prague and the sleepy lake town of Bled in Slovenia's Julian Alps.

It wasn't just sights; it was experiences like being serenaded in a winery in the Hungarian countryside by a feisty old (and good) violinist who brought tears to my eyes when he ended with *American the Beautiful*. (The wine might have had something to do with it.) Or Peter and I frantically trying to make the monumental decision of how to spend our last 400 florints before crossing from Hungary into Croatia. (We blew them all on a large Snickers bar.) Or eating all the fatty foods (like the grilled pig's knuckle in Prague) that we would never touch at home.

We've loved our respite from e-mail, the news of the world and the parade of decisions and worries of our daily life, but we're happy to be home.

December 13, 2015

FRUGAL PANAMA

It isn't every morning that you get up at 5:15 a.m. to milk cows on a farm that's a four-hour drive from Panama City, Panama. But nothing was off the table during our three days with the Seth in the tiny town of Santo Domingo, where, unlike most visitors to Panama, we never saw another American.

On a 100-degree day we visited the Belisario Porras Museum in Los Todas (50 cents entrance fee). In that oven-hot museum, Seth managed (as always) to make the guide love us, her first American visitors in a month. We visited Isla Iguana and other attractions on the Azuero Peninsula before heading to Panama City where we did normal stuff like visiting the Panama Canal and the new Frank Gehry Museum of Biodiversity.

This was the fifth time we joined Seth on his frugal travels. Each time we were thrilled to be able to go and we never took it for granted that we would be asked again. Nor did we take it for granted that we would be well enough to travel *his* way again.

It was especially poignant because he was turning in his Frugal Traveler badge and someone else would begin telling readers how to travel less expensively and more authentically. In his article about our trip, Seth wrote "My parents essentially taught me to travel, and we believe that being handed a baby (in Panama), getting a rental car stuck in the mud (Nicaragua), swimming with a local family (Croatia), happening upon a midsummer feast (Norway) or dining out in immigrant-filled suburbs (Vancouver) are the kind of experiences that matter more than museums and sightseeing cruises."

Our adventures with him will live on in the digital archives of *The New York Times*. And, more important, in our hearts.

April 3, 2016

NEW ORLEANS, LA

I haven't taken a vacation without Peter for almost fifty years. But when Jeremy and Katrina and our grandsons invited us to go with them to New Orleans for their spring break and Peter didn't want to go, I couldn't refuse. I'd never been there and I figured he'd be OK on his own for four days.

A million years ago, I had two roommates who had gone to school in New Orleans. I had heard about beignets and Bourbon Street. I had heard about brunch at Brennan's and Cajun cooking. But I'd never been there. All of the above still exist, plus the fabulous National World War II Museum

Joined by my sister-in-law, Nancy, we walked everywhere. The Easter Parade went on through intermittent downpours, but the rain didn't stop handfuls of beaded necklaces and fat raw carrots being thrown from the floats to the outstretched hands of onlookers. We walked Bourbon Street, Royal Street and Frenchman Street—jazz, galleries, pralines, crawfish—we tried everything. Our historic Hotel Le Pavillon served peanut butter and jelly sandwiches and hot chocolate with real whipped cream and marshmallows at 10:00 every night.

Leo and Jeremy walked 30,000 steps one day and the rest of us were pretty darn close. We went on a swamp tour. We saw *NCIS New Orleans* being filmed on St. Charles Street.

It was exhausting and wonderful. And Peter did fine.

July 14, 2016

THE CHATAUQUA INSTITUTION

We drove to western New York State for a one-week-vacation at the Chautauqua Institution. We'd heard good things about this 136-year-old "adult education center and summer resort" and thought it might suit us.

The theme for the week was "Money and Power." The Institute brought in a team of big names, including Bill Moyers, Steve Forbes and former Congressman Tim Roemer together with some not-so-big-names-but-very-smart-people like Zephyr Teachout and Mehrsa Baradaran who spoke on topics such as "How the Other Half Banks" (Baradaran) and Corruption (Teachout). A recurring theme was to get money out of politics.

What struck us as important was that these people did not just describe the problems. They suggested solutions.

There was also time for fun. The Capitol Steps, perfect satirists for an election year, mocked everyone in politics, and the crowd laughed uproariously. A concert by the Avett Brothers, a famous folk rock band, was a new (and very loud) experience for us, to say the least. The Chautauqua Symphony played. The Chautauqua Ballet danced. We couldn't do everything. It was exhausting.

The architecture of the Chautauqua "village" is wonderful. The gardens are gorgeous. We stayed in an old, paint-peeling hotel overlooking the lake. Our room had windows we could actually open.

When it was over, I needed a vacation.

August 7, 2016

THERE'S NO PLACE LIKE HOME

We'd been away quite a bit this summer, thanks to the generosity of friends with vacation homes and in spite of our own (slightly flagging) spirit of adventure.

There were weeks and weekends of no bread-like products (for gluten-intolerant me), no home delivered newspapers and in some cases, no cell-phone reception. Of course, we were more than compensated for all that by interesting people, new learning, and beautiful settings.

However, our own bed, our early morning newspapers, not having to ask if food is gluten-free and the return to our normal (for us) routine are comforting.

As travel dates approach, there's always a part of me that wishes we were home safe after a great trip. Once we get into the rhythm of being away, I don't think about that at all. But when we come home and my gluten-free bagel and my newspaper are on my breakfast table, I am relieved.

And grateful.

9
MARKING THE YEARS

BIRTHDAYS

"Do not regret growing older. It is a privilege denied to many."
Author Unknown

I love birthdays, mine and others'. I'll never forget my birthdays in Cincinnati where I lived from age four to nine. My mother and her friend Esther took my pal Barbara and me to lunch and an ice show at the Netherland Plaza Hotel every year. (The hotel still exists, but no more ice shows.)

I remember how excited I was for my first co-ed birthday party when I turned thirteen. Twelve of us had my mother's famous spaghetti with meat sauce for dinner at my house followed by duckpin bowling at our local alley.

I celebrated my 21st birthday at the Pretzel Bell in Ann Arbor, Michigan for my first legal beer(s) and my 50th at a Club Med in the Caribbean. And that's just a few of the good ones.

Stuffed in a desk drawer are all the birthday cards my kids have sent to me, including one from Seth, sent by his father before he was born. My birthdays (and sometimes Mother's Days) seem to be the time my children think of saying thank you for a job pretty well done by me. And they say it beautifully. The year that Jeremy became a father, he sent me a card on his birthday, congratulating me on being a good mother now that he understood what goes into being a parent

The kids expect that their cards will make me cry. I don't disappoint them.

Birthdays come around a little too quickly these days. But at least they come around.

February 21, 2008

How Do You "Look" 70?

I hadn't talked about my age much, except among friends and family. But I've decided that I'm 70, I'm ready to flaunt it.

I started with Kelly, who has been cutting my hair for over fifteen years. She's about 40 now. "No way" she exclaimed. "It can't be true!" Kathy, our trainer, sent me a card after I told her. She wrote, "no one would believe you are turning 70." Finally I told some people at work. Twenty-five year old Erin demanded my exercise program. Even the kids' friends were reportedly surprised.

So I ask this question? Who looks 70 and what makes anyone "look" that age? I have friends in their 70's, but I can't describe any shared characteristics like number of wrinkles or gray hair. I guess how one looks is more a reflection of attitude or behavior. Does my riding my bike to work or studying beginning Spanish make me look "not 70"?

A birthday card I received several years ago sits on the bulletin board above my desk. "It's not the years in your life, but the life in your years." So there was my answer—just waiting for me to notice it.

February 18, 2010

Birthday

I had my 72nd birthday yesterday. That means that I am one-fifth of the way to having to change the name of this blog to 80-something.com. And if the other eight years go as fast as the past two...

Birthdays make me think of other birthdays–like the one I had in college when my friends gave me a scavenger hunt with a gift certificate for a pint of ice cream from my favorite ice cream parlor at each site. I was in seventh heaven. Or the time we were out to dinner for my birthday with our good friends Gordon and Christa. I was reading the menu when the waiter appeared to take our order. I looked up and it was our son Seth who had driven from New York City for the weekend to surprise me. When we arrived at the restaurant, I had asked the maitre d' to take away the fifth chair because there were only four of us.

But yesterday's was a birthday I could easily forget. It started extra early when I drove Peter to the hospital to get a cataract removed. I dropped him there and rushed to work. I had an hour-long conference call I couldn't miss with people from Nigeria, Pakistan, and San Francisco—that's a lot of time zones to coordinate. I rushed back to the hospital to pick up Peter, took him home, and went back to work. Then I cooked my own birthday dinner.

Not the perfect birthday, but lots of cards and calls, and having Peter here with me—that all made it fine.

I am a lucky 72-year-old.

March 11, 2010

The 70-something Blogger's Spouse on Turning Eighty

Guest Commentary:

Today is my eightieth birthday, and I am beginning to feel old. I didn't feel old at seventy. I had a full-time job. I was biking long distances on summer vacations, and I only took one pill in the morning. Now, ten years later, I'm retired, I take about ten pills a day, and seldom bike more than two miles.

Don't get me wrong. I'm still happy to be on this side of the grass. I'm happy to wake up next to Judy. I'm happy to learn something new almost every day. I'm happy when I hear Mozart or come up with a new idea. And I still like managing the things I run.

So far so good. But I wonder how I'll feel when I turn ninety. If I turn ninety.

I'd like to turn ninety, and keep going because there are still lots of things I'd like to do. I want to see what happens to my children and grandchildren. I have things I'd like to teach, some research problems I'd like to solve and a martini or two I'd like to drink.

Although ordinarily, I don't like being interrupted while I'm in the middle of doing something, that's how I'd like to go—while I'm in the middle of doing something. But, as Saint Augustine said after he asked his God for chastity, not yet.

May 23, 2010

Our First-Born Turns Forty

At 6:15 this morning we drove our son Seth to the airport. He lives in Brazil and we hadn't seen him since Thanksgiving. He was home for a total of eighteen hours, and if you subtract sleeping, we had a total of eleven hours with him. Better than nothing, but never enough.

On Saturday he will turn forty. How can that be? Weren't Peter and I just recently referring to the occupant of my belly as "Pumpkinella" or "Pinocchio"? Wasn't it recently that I declared that he would never be allowed to cross the street alone and that he would be home-schooled through college?

We had a great visit. We had lunch on the patio on a gorgeous June-like day. We went for a long walk. I cooked one of his favorite meals for dinner. We talked about his next assignment.

Just before he arrived, the mailman had delivered a disk I had had made of four hundred photos from our wedding through our grandchildren's births and we watched the slide show of our lives together.

And then, this morning, he was gone.

February 17, 2011

Birthday

Today I turned seventy-three. I used to think seventy-three was old, but now I know better.

Growing up, I was the youngest in my class because I started kindergarten at age four. My mother had begged the Cincinnati Board of Education to let me start school early because we had just moved there, I had no friends, and I did have four weeks of kindergarten under my belt from Buffalo, New York where school started at four for everyone.

I have a vague recollection of the test the Board of Education gave me. I remember a picture of two baby shoes and I was asked what was missing. Well, one of the shoes had no laces. Much to my mother's relief, the Board of Education allowed me to enter kindergarten.

As the youngest, I was the last one of my friends to get a driver's license, vote and drink legally. Back then I was always wishing that I was older.

No more. Today, on my seventy-third birthday, one of my close childhood classmates is already seventy-four years and four days old. Two others will be celebrating their seventy-fourth birthdays soon. All three of these women are living proof that seventy-three can be a very good age, and I'm counting on that.

Peter asked me what I would like for my birthday.

"Nothing money can buy," I told him.

March 10, 2011

EIGHTY-ONE AND COUNTING

Today is Peter's eighty-first birthday. In addition to making me very happy for forty-six years, he has made me recalibrate what it means to be old. Sure he's wrinkly and a little bit stooped (I do recall his amazing posture when we met—compared to my life-long slump). Sure he has several pretty serious ailments, including Parkinson's disease, glaucoma, and more. But this man is about as upbeat as they come.

The other day I asked him why he seemed so happy. I wanted to know why he can make me laugh every day. And why he works so hard at staying well despite his health challenges. He tells me he has a good life. His mind is working just fine (although he would say not as quickly) and he is engaged in several activities that require him to use it. He works out extensively every day (he is pretty sure that exercise is crucial to his well-being). And I know he gets pleasure from seeing me happy.

Lest you think he is too perfect, he gets irritated with me when I interrupt him, his desk is a mess, and he is never happy when I remind him to get a much-needed haircut.

My father always used to kid my mother—telling her at age fifty that he was going to trade her in for two twenty-five year olds. Fortunately for all of us, (including the twenty-five year olds) that never happened.

Would I trade Peter for two forty and a half year olds?

Not on your life.

February 17, 2013

SUMMING UP SEVENTY-FOUR

Today is my seventy-fifth birthday. It's just another day. It's just another year. But somehow it feels different. I've been around for three-quarters of a century—that's a long time.

I'm lucky. I still have the love of my life. I have great children and grandchildren and I'm happily employed. Although I have a knee that is not my own, my health is excellent. OK, last week the eye doctor said my eyes are showing signs of aging. But so is the rest of me.

Over the past year, I've come to see myself as an older person. A 70-something reader once commented that life is a conveyor belt, and eventually we come to the end. It seems closer now.

The other day my former boss was in town and he dropped by my office. He is twelve years younger than I am, but took early retirement four years ago. When asked "What's new?" I told him that I was about to be seventy-five.

"That makes me happy," he replied. "I wasn't looking forward to being seventy-five, but when I see you, I know it's going to be OK."

It is.

February 21, 2013

BIRTHDAY

I wasn't excited about turning seventy-five. I would have been happy to put it off for, let's say, a decade. On the other hand, it would be a non-Thanksgiving opportunity to get everyone in the family together.

Despite the bitter cold and freezing winds in New York City last weekend, I had one of the best birthdays of my life.

I was not involved in the planning. I know it wasn't easy. The grandchildren in Maryland had to get out of school early, their parents had to battle DC's Beltway and the Holland Tunnel in a long-weekend traffic jam, and our always-traveling son had to fit in some time between trips to Korea and Brazil. But somehow it all came together.

We stayed in a très chic hotel next to the High Line, a park created from a once-to-be-demolished elevated train track, in New York's (also) très chic meatpacking district. Our rooms had Hudson River views from their floor-to-ceiling windows. My only request had been to see the 9/11 Memorial so we joined the throngs of people paying their respects at the World Trade Center on a cold, gray Saturday morning.

Eating is a high priority for our family, and we did a lot of that. Walking is important when you do a lot of eating so we did a lot of that too, only using cabs or the subway or ducking into a Whole Foods market when frostbite threatened.

But what really matters is that the weekend reassured me that I haven't done such a bad job of being a wife, mother, colleague and friend. There were a lot of tears (all mine), as I made an individual toast to each member of my beloved family at our Saturday night, adults-only dinner. There were more tears (still all mine) at my Sunday birthday lunch over my present, *75 Twitter-Length Tributes to Judy Kugel* from friends, family and colleagues.

I will treasure it for as long as I have birthdays.

January 11, 2015

Happy Birthday to the 70-something Blog

Yesterday was the seventh anniversary of 70-something.com. That means that, in a little over a month, I will be seventy-seven years old. This is my 737th post, and I am arrogant (audacious, cocky, presumptuous?) enough to think that I still have something to say. True (sadly), I am not the same person that I was on January 10, 2007.

I'm definitely more vulnerable. I worry even more about Peter who is amazing, but approaching eighty-five. I'm retired and that is huge. Our grandchildren are real people now. They laugh with us and at us, unlike when they were one and four. The world still has many challenges, but that will never change.

And so do I (have challenges), but I plan to do my best, and I hope you will stick with me.

Thanks for reading.

February 22, 2015

BIRTHDAY REPORT

Tuesday was my seventy-seventh birthday. I wasn't especially looking forward to it. But I wasn't *not* looking forward to it either. It's not like "Whoopie, now I can drive or drink or vote." Those were the birthdays that really mattered.

What I can do at seventy-seven is be grateful that I made it to here in good health and that I have a life full of family and friends.

On Tuesday, I heard from everybody. The grandchildren and their parents sang Happy Birthday over the phone. Seth called while rushing around to leave on assignment to Georgia and Armenia. A former roommate that I hadn't heard from in more than a year called. My brother called. Aunt Ruth, age 103, called.

Of course, Peter treated me like queen-for-a-day.

After all that excitement, I am relieved that it's twelve months 'til the next one.

March 12, 2015

CELEBRATING PETER

The Kugel family met in New York City last weekend to celebrate Peter's 85th birthday. Although Peter doesn't like being the center of attention, he had no choice.

I took care of theater tickets and dinner arrangements, but Seth and Jeremy created the Peter Kugel Family Feud, an experience we will talk about for years. They sent multiple-choice questionnaires to a hundred of their friends and ours. Questions included, "What part of *The New York Times* does Peter turn to first?" "If Peter were an animal, what would he be?" "What trait have Seth and Jeremy inherited most from Peter?" Somehow they got the real Family Feud TV show board on Seth's large computer monitor. It was completely true-to-life, with Jeremy starring as host Richard Dawson.

No gift could have better expressed the love of our two sons for their amazing father.

February 19, 2017

How Seventy-Nine Feels

I've been seventy-nine for two days. So far, so good. I'm very aware that I'm lucky to be here and even luckier to have my wonderful family and friends on this journey with me.

Lately, however, I have been thinking about how different I am now than I was nine years ago. In the first half of this decade, my job defined who I was as much as my family. That certainly changed. Though I have a busy and fulfilling retirement, I miss my work community. I don't want to be there, but I still miss it.

Many other things have changed. My cell phone was a clamshell then, and now it is a computer. Our grandchildren were toddlers and now they are so much fun to talk to and hang out with. We're a little slower at just about everything we do, but we still "do".

And, as always, I am so grateful that I have Peter. For my birthday, he bought me my favorite flowers and a gadget that I can't explain, but that should help us produce some interesting (and healthy) deserts.

Because I started kindergarten a year younger than my classmates, my high school and college friends are turning 80 this year. I'm keeping an eye on them to see what lies ahead.

10

HOW WE ARE REMEMBERED

LEGACY

"Don't judge each day by the harvest you reap,
but by the seeds that you plant."
Robert Louis Stevenson

How will we be remembered? And what do we want to be remembered for? As young and middle-aged adults, we probably weren't thinking about our legacy, even though we were building it every day. At 70-something it's on our minds.

It's tempting to believe that our legacy has been determined, but every day we have the opportunity to reinforce it and/or to add to it. Living in the moment, taking care of loved ones, giving back now that we are (mostly) retired. As Meg Newhouse asks in her recent book, *Legacies of the Heart,* "Have we left the world a little better than we found it?"

From Generation to Generation

Several years ago, Jeremy asked Peter and me to write about our lives up to the time he was born. So write we did. We enjoyed trying to capture the essence of our growing up and the patterns of behavior we developed that made us who we are today, for better or for worse.

Both of our hastily written autobiographies of "the early years" ended up to be seventeen single-spaced pages long. We were astonished to learn things about each other from reading about each other's lives before we met.

Then last spring, Jeremy asked us to talk about where we are in our lives on videotape. The plan was that the tape would be embargoed for twenty years when it would be played for our grandchildren.

Jeremy set up the camera on the porch, saying he would be back in 15 minutes and instructed me to talk. By the time he came back, I was reduced to tears, saying how much I loved everyone to the video camera. Then it was Peter's turn. I have no idea what he said, but I do know that he had more trouble filling the 15 minutes than I did, typical silent-male type that he is.

I often wish I could talk to my parents these days. I want to know what they were thinking at my age. How did they feel about turning 70? I want to know more about my father's difficult childhood. I want to know if my mother ever wished that she had had a career other than as a mom. I wonder if she had that empty feeling in the pit of her stomach that I always have when a child leaves after a visit home.

Through our writing about our early lives and our recording about where we are now, our children will have answers to some of the questions I wish I could ask my parents. And maybe, just maybe, our grandkids will tell their own children what life was like for their grandparents at the turn of the 21st century.

May 5, 2008

We have two grandsons, age 4 and 1½. They are perfect. We have just reconfirmed that fact on a weekend visit. Sadly, they don't live nearby, so we only get to see them every few months. But I want them to know us as I never got to know my own grandparents. I want them to see in writing how much we love them. So each time we see them, I write them a "letter" about how they have grown and changed, how proud we are of them and how much joy they brings us.

I also tell them about us. For example after Peter's retirement party a couple of years ago, I "wrote" to them. I told them how I had learned things about their grandfather that night that I never knew. About his accomplishments in his field, about his kindnesses, about how his students loved him. About how they named a room after him at Boston College. Even the grandkids' father and uncle were saying," Wow, we never knew that about Dad!"

Today I will write about Leo's incredible knowledge of the Boston Red Sox and how he beat me at basketball. I will write about how he talks non-stop. I will write about his little brother's irresistible belly laugh, how he loves to be chased, how he is saying really understandable words like bubble and purple and juice.

I will tell them what a great job their parents are doing with them and that I cannot wait to hug them both again.

June 10, 2010

I have been writing "letters" to our grandchildren since Leo, our first, was born six years ago. I want them to be able to read about how much we loved watching them grow. And I tell them some things about us because if we are lucky enough to see them grown up, we won't be what we used to be.

Here is part of my latest letter.

"It was three months since we had seen you, and you have changed, as you always do. But this time, we realized that Grady is no longer a toddler. At three and a half, Grady, you are a force. Funny, full of sentences, a Superman in every sense of the phrase, especially in your Superman P.J.'s complete with cape. What is so amazing is that although you guys are two and a half years apart, you're great friends. At least most of the time. Grady looks up to you, Leo, and you take care of him. Most of the time. And most nights Grady joins you by sleeping in the top bunk in your room.

What made this weekend special is that we took care of you without your parents for twenty-five hours. You were on your best behavior except when Grady wanted to go to the "treeless tree house," and we thought that was off limits.

When you and I were reading a counting book together, Grady, we realized it had been in the mud, and I had a lot of dirt from it on my Capri pants. I wiped it away with my hands, but you kept finding more and brushing it away. It was a small moment, but one I will treasure. And I'll treasure seeing you, Leo, so tall and slender, fitting into your mother's roller blades at age six. You're not too confident on them, but you're getting there.

We had a good time before Mommy and Daddy left, and after they came home, but the very best was when we got to substitute for them, reading to you and then cuddling with you in the bunk beds at bed time."

How sweet it was!

January 12, 2012

How Do We Want to be Remembered?

I always thought that legacies were people who got into college because a parent or older sibling was a graduate. Until lately.

Since I became a grandparent, I've been thinking about my own legacy, how I want to be remembered. For eight years, I have been writing letters to our grandchildren. They don't live near us, so I generally write them when we come home from a visit. I tell them about us and about them and how they have changed.

They won't see the letters until they (and we) are much older, but there will be a record of those magic moments of getting to know them, a legacy of sorts.

A few years ago, our son Jeremy videotaped Peter and me separately on his front porch, each talking about our life and our times to be shown to the grandkids in twenty years. So, thanks to their father, they will have our faces as well as our words.

How I wish I had something like that from my parents! What I would give to have their reflections on their lives when they were the age I am now.

On Monday, thanks to a newspaper article by Jane Brody, I read a review of a new book about legacy called *Thirty Lessons for Living: Tried and True Advice from the Wisest Americans*. The book summarizes the views of more than 1,000 Americans as compiled by the Cornell Legacy Project. Topics include Aging, Marriage, Parenting, Careers and more as viewed by more than 1,000 older Americans.

A legacy that can benefit us right now.

January 4, 2015

Legacy—an update from PK

I'm going to be eighty-five in March and according to the conventional wisdom, that's a big deal. I'll be "old-old" after ten years of being "young-old." Looks like it's time to think about my legacy.

Our sons and grandsons who live far away are a big part of that legacy. We talk to them more via electronic gadgets than face-to-face. Seth, our older son is in Brazil working on a book and going to the beach. When he was in New York City in December writing, directing and starring in his zany "Amigo Gringo" videos, he told us that he now (very occasionally) listens to Mozart on vinyl, as his parents did when he was a child.

Jeremy, our younger son, is in Maryland trying to keep a school financially solvent. Today our grandsons Leo and Grady will get the dog they've been wishing for forever and Katrina will soon have a new kitchen. Jeremy will continue–but hopefully not complete–his attempt to eat in the 100 most-successful food chains in America.

They're our legacy. I'll be sorry to leave them, but while I am still on this side of the grass, they make me smile.

AFTERWORD

I am fortunate to have lived beyond the three score and ten years that the Bible tells us to expect. And writing the 70-something.com blog has helped me understand this stage of my life.

When you write, you notice. I find more joy in nature, a good book and a good interaction when I write about them.

I have become better at accepting change and distinguishing the small things from the things that matter. I have become better about appreciating what I can still do rather than bemoaning what I can't.

My seventies have been bonus years in every sense of the word and I have tried to appreciate that every day—a habit I hope to continue into my eighties.

And beyond.

As one reader wrote,
"Judy gets what I'm feeling."
Subscribe and follow her
posts regularly at:

www.70-something.com

About the Author

Judy Kugel retired as Associate Dean of Students at Harvard's John F. Kennedy School of Government in 2013. She has counseled people making career and life choices since 1970 when she co-founded the Boston Project for Careers, a nonprofit organization that developed opportunities for men and women who were seeking part-time jobs, often after being at home with young children. The Boston Project for Careers was one of the first organizations to promote job-sharing for professionals.

Her personal essays and travel articles have appeared in magazines and major newspapers including *The New York Times* and *The Boston Globe*. She has explored life transitions throughout her career and led several workshops on that subject. An avid writer of journals, she went public in 2008, when she started her twice-weekly blog at www.70-something. com

In her "retirement," she is a consultant, a coach, a blogger and a grandmother (in reverse order of importance).

A graduate of the University of Michigan with a B.A. in Political Science, she received a M.Ed. in Counseling Psychology from Boston College.

Made in the USA
San Bernardino, CA
01 June 2017